*In Search of a National Landscape*
WILLIAM TROST RICHARDS
AND THE ARTISTS' ADIRONDACKS, 1850–1870

*William T. Richards painting at Lake Placid*, 1904
Photograph taken by his daughter Eleanor Richards Price (1862–1954)
Collection of David and Inge Price

# In Search of a National Landscape

## WILLIAM TROST RICHARDS

## AND THE ARTISTS' ADIRONDACKS, 1850–1870

ESSAYS BY

LINDA S. FERBER

AND

CAROLINE M. WELSH

*THE ADIRONDACK MUSEUM*

BLUE MOUNTAIN LAKE, N.Y. 12812

Cover: *In the Adirondacks,* 1857 (cat. no. 11)
Oil on canvas 29 x 43 1/2
Signed and dated l.l. Wm T. Richards/1857.
The Adirondack Museum 69.53.1 (211)

Copy Editor: Fronia W. Simpson
Project Director and Associate Editor: Caroline M. Welsh
Indexed by: Frances Bowles

Production Coodinator: Elizabeth Folwell
Designer: Lisa Richmond
Photographers: Richard Walker and Erik Borg

Library of Congress Control Number:   2002106628

Printed by: Queen City Printers Inc.

ISBN 0-910020-47-7

# CONTENTS

*Autumn in the Adirondacks,* 1865 (cat. no. 29)
Oil on canvas 25 x 36
Signed, dated, and inscribed l.r. Wm. T. Richards/Phila. 1865
Kenneth Lux Gallery

# PREFACE

THE ADIRONDACK MUSEUM is located at the center of the Adirondack Park, a vast mosaic of state and private land that comprises the largest public park in the contiguous United States. Since 1894, nearly half of the Adirondack Park's six million acres have been protected as "forever wild" by the New York State constitution. The changing face of the Adirondacks as a wilderness place is one of the central themes of The Adirondack Museum.

Since the museum opened to the public in 1957, its exhibitions and publications have documented the complex interaction between people and the land as well as cultural attitudes toward nature. The American experience of the wilderness has been in part defined in this region, where the reality of everyday life and work was transformed through the myth-making imagination of its artists, among them, William Trost Richards and his contemporary artists of the 1850s and 1860s.

This exhibition and publication present for the first time a focused look at William Trost Richards's Adirondack art and the role that Adirondack imagery played in his creative output. We are indebted to the scholarship of the art historian and Richards scholar Linda S. Ferber, who has given generously of her knowledge and research to bring the fruits of her work to this museum. Caroline M. Welsh, Chief Curator and Curator of Art, has made significant contributions to the scholarship of Adirondack art and to the art collection of The Adirondack Museum. She has led museum staff and consultants with great energy and commitment to bring this important study to the public through these two exhibitions: *In Search of a National Landscape: William Trost Richards in the Adirondacks* and *"A wild yet pleasing landscape": The Artists' Adirondacks, 1850–1870.*

John R. Collins
Director

# ACKNOWLEDGMENTS

THE ADIRONDACK MUSEUM'S mission to collect, preserve, and interpret the history of the Adirondack region affords us a unique opportunity to examine regional characteristics and adaptations in relation to their national context. We have used our art collection in particular to study images of Adirondack scenery and artists' interpretation of it in terms of American art on a national scale. To this end we have studied Winslow Homer, Arthur Fitzwilliam Tait, Levi Wells Prentice, Rockwell Kent, and now William Trost Richards. Each of these artists is renowned in American art and each made Adirondack subject matter a serious part of his artistic work.

We are most grateful to the Richards scholar Linda S. Ferber. Dr. Ferber has been more than a guest curator for this project. Since 1995 she has served on the museum's art committee and has made many contributions to enhancing and understanding this fine collection, the single largest repository of images of the Adirondacks. The Andrew W. Mellon Curator of American Art at the Brooklyn Museum of Art, Ferber is a scholar of American art. She began her study of William Trost Richards in graduate school, and her dissertation was the first major examination of Richards's life and career. She has organized further exhibitions and written catalogues that appeared in 1973, 1982, 1986, and 2001. Her encyclopedic knowledge, along with her flair for detective work, has resulted in a treasure trove of Adirondack drawings and paintings from the beginning, middle, and end of this artist's career. The study of Adirondack art is as enriched by Ferber's scholarship as we at The Adirondack Museum are by her generosity and friendship.

There are many people and institutions to thank for their assistance with this exhibition. The generosity of the lenders is paramount; without their cooperation and support there would be no exhibit. Various members of the staff participated and supported this project at all its stages: Tracy Meehan, collections manager, Angela Donnelly, assitant registrar, and Doreen Alessi, conservator, are deserving of special mention. The exhibition has benefited from the support and individual generosity of the Board of Trustees. The curators are especially grateful to Trustee Andrew Lack for his belief in the project and his personal support of the exhibition catalog. We are indebted to Lisa Richmond for its handsome design and production, to Elizabeth Folwell for coordinating production, and to Fronia W. Simpson for her graceful and intelligent editing of our work.

Caroline M. Welsh
Chief Curator and Curator of Art

I MUST ADD MY OWN THANKS to those of John Collins and Caroline Welsh for the tremendous support offered by dozens and dozens of well-wishers to this ambitious project. My heartfelt gratitude goes first and foremost to the lenders for their extraordinary patience, cooperation, and generosity, especially the members of the artist's family. I am equally indebted to the staff and trustees of The Adirondack Museum who have been steadfast in their enthusiasm for this long-planned project. The Chief Curator and Curator of Art, Caroline Welsh, has been my co-curator and supporter, always gracious and always on time! She and Peter Welsh have also been great partners (and often hosts) for many Adirondack research expeditions since we began to plan this exhibition and publication in 1994. Special thanks go to Jerold Pepper, who patiently guided me through the research treasures of the museum's library and archives, and to Tracy Meehan for her good work in the registrar's office.

Other individuals and institutions have been very generous over the years in offering assistance of many kinds to my work. I can thank here only a few who have helped bring to light William Trost Richards's contribution to the canon of Adirondack landscape images. They include Alexander Acevedo, Alexander Gallery; Michael Altman, Altman Fine Arts; Dr. Richard D. Bullock; Joseph S. Caldwell IV, Caldwell Gallery; John Driscoll, Babcock Gallery; Martha Fleischman, Kennedy Galleries, Inc.; Debra Force, Debra Force Fine Arts; Betsy G. Fryberger, Iris & B. Gerald Cantor Center for Visual Arts, Stanford University; James Berry Hill and Frederick Hill, Berry-Hill Galleries, Inc.; Laura Guarisco, Guarisco Gallery Ltd.; Sarah E. Kelly; Alison E. Ledes, *The Magazine Antiques*; Arnold L. Lehman, Marilyn S. Kushner, Antoinette Owen, and Rachel Danzig, Brooklyn Museum of Art; Kenneth Lux, Kenneth Lux Fine Arts; Dr. Kenneth Maddox, The Newington-Cropsey Foundation; Dr. Angela Miller, Washington University; Merl M. Moore Jr.; Kenneth S. Moser; M. P. Naud, Hirschl & Adler Galleries; Jill Newhouse; the late Mrs. Emmet N. O'Brien and William K. Verner; Robin Pell; Inge and David Price; Irma Rudin; Robert Schwarz, The Schwarz Gallery; Ira Spanierman, Spanierman Gallery LLC; David Trout; William Vareika, William Vareika Fine Arts; Eric Widing and Megan E. Holloway, Christie's; and Deedee Wigmore, D. Wigmore Fine Arts. A very special debt of gratitude is due to James Bailey, City Historian of Plattsburgh, New York, who has been our greatest resource in identifying the locations in Richards's Adirondack paintings.

Linda S. Ferber

# INTRODUCTION
## *Linda S. Ferber*

I N 1873 *THE ALDINE*, a popular magazine devoted to art and literature, counted William Trost Richards (1833–1905) among the important interpreters of Adirondack scenery: "For the past thirty years this region of country has been a favorite resort for artists. A. B. Durand, J. W. Casilear, and J. F. Kensett led the way, being followed in 1855, by J. M. Hart, and in 1863 by W. T. Richards, all of whom found plenty of material for many of their finest sketches."[1] Today, Richards is principally recognized as a painter of marine and coastal subjects, whose career flourished during the last quarter of the nineteenth century. Less well known is the fact that during his early practice, from 1853 to 1870, his primary subject was the American landscape, participating at midcentury in the collective artistic project to originate a landscape vision that might be acknowledged as national.

Richards's experience in the Adirondacks played a critical role in this development; and much earlier in actuality than reported in *The Aldine*, for Richards had first explored New York State and the Adirondack region in 1855. He returned in 1857 and, possibly, again in 1859. We know that he was there in 1862, 1863, 1865, perhaps 1866, and in 1868. From studies made on these forays, Richards produced a series of paintings that figure among the most beautiful and significant records of the region produced at midcentury. Decades later, in the summer of 1904, he returned to paint a striking series of plein-air oil studies while vacationing at Lake Placid with his daughter and fellow artist Anna Richards Brewster (1870–1952).

Richards's encounters with the region came at critical moments both in his own career and in the life of the nation. The Adirondack region provided a virtual laboratory in which he worked out various landscape agendas over more than a decade. These ranged from the mastery of the mainstream Hudson River School style in the 1850s to experimentation with an extreme realism that established him in the 1860s as a central figure in the short-lived and controversial American Pre-Raphaelite movement. His first Adirondack campaigns of the late 1850s took place at the high-water mark of the Hudson River, or New York, School's mission to define a national landscape. These Adirondack paintings effectively launched Richards's career (cat. nos. 11–14). At the same moment, however, sectional tensions and political strife were changing cultural attitudes to landscape that signaled the beginning of the school's decline, a trend accelerated by the Civil War and its aftermath. Richards's Adirondack campaigns of the 1860s, conducted during and after the Civil War, occurred in a different context. The commanding optimism of Manifest Destiny was briefly deferred to the pressing need to seek a landscape of both personal and national reconciliation. From this necessity, I will argue, a subtly different landscape vision emerged (cat. nos. 21–30).

In 1904 Richards's final return to paint these mountains, long after his reputation and market had been confirmed as a marine painter, demonstrated the powerful associations the region continued to hold for him and his generation. The Lake Placid plein-air studies of light and atmosphere, grounded in the same empirical investigation of regional topography that inform the pencil drawings from his early forays, are among the freshest and most beautiful paintings of a remarkably vigorous old age.

The Adirondack wilderness was the northernmost outpost in a landscape itinerary that extended south along the narrow mountain valley course of the Hudson River to the more familiar and accessible touring and sketching grounds of the Catskills, the Hudson Highlands, and the Palisades. The Adirondack mountain range in northeastern New York State is bounded by Lakes George to the south and east and Champlain to the north and east. On the west lies the Black River and the Tug Hill Plateau.[2] This is the region in which Thomas Cole (1801–1848) had found the "wildness" described in his 1835 "Essay on American Scenery" as "perhaps the most impressive characteristic of American scenery."[3] Asher B. Durand (1796–1886) had found his calling as a landscape painter in these mountains on an 1837 expedition with Cole to Schroon Lake. The rich language of Durand's "Letters on Landscape Painting," published in 1855 just as Richards was planning his Adirondack expedition, gives us insight into the powerful associations, always on the edge of transcendence, that were invested in the landscape experience. Durand also saw the whole artistic project of American landscape painting as uniquely expressive of both national and cultural identity.[4] Richards's own declarations indicate that he shared this point of view. "Really Annie," he wrote to his new bride from Coldspring on the Hudson in 1857, "the best thing in the world is to be a good conscientious painter. . . . I never commence anything without an earnest prayer for God's help."[5]

Like Durand and Cole, Richards was particularly drawn to Essex County, bounded on the east by Lake Champlain and containing within its boundaries the highest Adirondack peaks as well as the source of the Hudson River (see fig. 4). Essex County also contains some of the region's most dramatic geologic and glacial formations. The more hospitable terrains of Pleasant Valley and neighboring Keene Valley were also favorite sketching grounds of the period.

While Richards's regular sojourns preceded the tourist explosion of the 1870s, the Adirondack region was already established by 1855 as a destination for the hardy excursionist. As we see from the paintings of Cole and Durand, Adirondack subjects, enhanced by historical and literary associations, already operated as part of a national canon of American landscape images. Elizabethtown, the county seat where Richards seems to have been based on his visits, was a regional crossroads during the years 1850 to 1870 for many artists in search of a national landscape. Their quest is the subject of this volume.

NOTES

1. "Elizabeth Valley," *The Aldine* 6 (October 1873): 198.

2. For a general history of the region, see Alfred L. Donaldson, *A History of the Adirondacks*, 2 vols. (New York: The Century Co., 1921; reprint, Mamaroneck, N.Y.: Harbor Hill Books, 1977).

3. Thomas Cole, "Essay on American Scenery," *American Monthly Magazine*, n.s., 1 (January 1836): 1–12; reprinted in John W. McCoubrey, *American Art, 1700–1900: Sources and Documents* (Englewood, N.J.: Prentice-Hall, 1965), 102; hereafter cited as Cole, "Essay" (1835).

4. The nine articles, published between January and July, demonstrate in their earnest eloquence the highly charged state in which American scenery and landscape painting were approached by artists, critics, and audience at midcentury. There can be little doubt that Richards knew these important documents; hereafter cited as Durand, "Letters" (1855).

5. Richards to Anna M. Richards, Coldspring, New York, [August] 1857, private collection.

*The Bouquet Valley, Adirondacks*, 1866 ( cat. no. 30)
Oil on canvas 25 x 42
Signed, dated, and inscribed l.l. Wm T. Richards/Phil. 1866
Biggs Museum of American Art

Fig. 1. *William T. Richards*, ca. 1855
Photographer unknown. Private collection

# In Search of a National Landscape
## WILLIAM TROST RICHARDS
### in the Adirondacks

LINDA S. FERBER

*Mountains of the Mind: Early Life, Education, and Influences*

Richards was born and raised in Philadelphia. His formal education at Central High School was terminated in 1847 by his father's death, requiring him as the eldest son to go to work.[1] He was employed as a draftsman and designer of ornamental metalwork for a local manufacturer of lamps and chandeliers. Nevertheless, Richards also pursued his higher ambitions to be a landscape painter (fig. 1). One local landscape specialist was of particular importance in these early years. The German expatriate Paul Weber (1823–1916) was a well-trained painter whose landscapes earned critical praise and wide patronage from the time of his arrival in Philadelphia in 1848 until he returned to Germany in 1860. During the decade of his residency, Weber was also an important teacher, offering instruction to Richards and his contemporaries who included Edward Moran (1829–1901), William Stanley Haseltine (1835–1900), and Edmund Darch Lewis (1835–1910).[2] Richards's art studies with Weber were conducted on a part-time and informal basis. His mentor's mountain subjects, grounded in a Northern European vision and style of painting, were among Richards's earliest visual models (fig. 2). Whereas Weber sketched among the mountain ranges of Pennsylvania, New Hampshire, and New York, his young pupil was locally bound to sketching forays near Philadelphia and

Fig. 2. *Mount Washington from the Saco*, 1854
Paul Weber (1823–1916). Oil on canvas 25 1/2 x 37. Private collection

Germantown. Lengthier expeditions were limited to a few vacation weeks in the summers. In 1851 Richards traveled west to the rolling farmlands of Chester County, and in 1852, north to Pennsylvania's Wyoming Valley, probably his first experience with mountainous terrain.

Richards also continued his intellectual and academic education with self-study and by maintaining contact with high school friends through a Literary and Forensic Circle, whose members were devoted to the practice of debate, public speaking, and composing essays and

poetry. A deep familiarity with American and English literature and poetry would continue to enrich Richards's responses to natural scenery over a lifetime. He participated eagerly in the culture of the picturesque, and the exalted language of his essays informed his letters as well. Indeed, Richards's knowledge of and response to mountain imagery and symbolism can be gleaned from language in these early letters and literary efforts. He was keenly sensitive to all suggestions of higher significance in natural phenomena, sharing the belief that contemplation of nature inspired perception of great truths. Long before his actual on-site experience among the high peaks of New York State, or any other alpine terrain, mountain forms loomed large in Richards's consciousness, as they did in the collective imagination of the period.

Mountains signaled both religious and aesthetic transcendence. They were the natural seat of the "Terrible Sublime" in British and American aesthetic discourse.[3] Mountains figured as emblems of spiritual challenge on the way to the Celestial City in John Bunyan's *The Pilgrim's Progress from This World to That Which Is to Come* (1678). The perennially popular prose allegory was a pervasive metaphor in literary and common parlance at midcentury, even providing the subject for public entertainment in the form of a moving panorama. As a vividly imagined narrative of Christian piety and morality, *The Pilgrim's Progress* was also a favorite subject for artists in the 1840s and 1850s. The allegory inspired paintings by Thomas Cole, Daniel Huntington (1816–1906), Frederic Edwin Church (1826–1900), and Jasper Cropsey (1823–1900), as well as the Philadelphians Peter F. Rothermel (1817–1895), Isaac L. Williams (1817–1895), and Richards himself. The titles of his earliest paintings include subjects from Bunyan, *The House Called Beautiful* (his 1852 debut at the Pennsylvania Academy of the Fine Arts) and more than one version of *The Delectable Mountains*.[4] In fact, Richards often cast himself as a pilgrim making his way over the difficult terrain of life's challenges. In a letter of 1854 regarding his favorite subject from Bunyan, Richards imagined himself as the protagonist: "As to myself, I hope soon to commence climbing the Delectable Mountains. . . . I fear it will be as perilous [an] ascent to me, as that of Mount Blanc is to some."[5] Asher B. Durand would also employ the mountain-climbing metaphor to demonstrate the rigors of career building in his final "Letter on Landscape."[6]

Mountains were also enlisted for political agendas. The Presidential Range of the White Mountains in New Hampshire signaled such a transfer of patriotic meaning onto landscape, transforming dramatic topography into a series of national monuments. At midcentury mountains were also recognized as dramatic testimony to the earth's long prehistory and formation by the operations of geologic process, rather than according to biblical account.[7] We know that Richards partici-

pated in the public fascination with geologic phenomena. His early interest is documented in a letter of 1854 to James Mitchell, a high school friend studying at Harvard, where the faculty included the charismatic Swiss scientist and educator Louis Agassiz, whose books and popular lectures helped to establish geology as a favorite amateur pastime in the United States. "I almost envy your geological Surveys with Prof. Agassiz," Richards wrote from Philadelphia, "I have long been wishing to study in an Elementary Manner Geology. Can you tell me of any thoroughly good book; I must make it part of my discipline for the winter."[8]

Richards was also responding to the new set of demands made on the modern landscape painter to understand and delineate the operation of geologic and meteorologic processes that shape the earth's surface. Landscape study was being redefined from the mastery of a picturesque vocabulary based on old master precedents to the documentation of a system of natural forces at work in an endless process of eruption and erosion. John Ruskin (1819–1900), another of Richards's heroes, was an avid amateur geologist who would devote the entire fourth volume of *Modern Painters* (1856) to the topic "Of Mountain Beauty."[9] An article in *The Crayon* of 1859, "Relation between Geology and Landscape Painting," demonstrates the midcentury alignment of landscape imagery and scientific inquiry into the earth's history: "[The landscape painter] meets with immense fissures and volcanoes, and he asks himself whence did they originate and by what convulsion were they produced? To him, therefore, properly belongs the study of geology, as he more thoroughly than any other can imitate what nature has produced."[10] The Adirondacks offered both artist and scientist a virtual laboratory for such study.

Richards's attention to geologic specificity would be reinforced in the 1860s by his involvement with the American Pre-Raphaelite circle, where his fellows included the geologists Clarence King and James F. Gardner.[11] Richards made careful drawings and paintings of alpine terrain and glaciers on the European trips of the middle 1850s and 1860s that bracket the Adirondack campaigns under investigation here (fig. 3). Long after his focus had shifted to marine subjects, Richards's

Fig. 3. *Rosenlaui Valley and the Wetterhorn*, 1858
William T. Richards (1833–1905). Oil on canvas 41 x 32
Private collection, Atlanta, Ga.

been his initial firsthand experience with the visual drama of the mountain-river-valley prospect, a configuration that would figure prominently in his Adirondack paintings. Although no drawings or paintings of the region by Richards have been located, a letter he wrote to Mitchell captures his landscape experiences in a series of vivid images: "Fortunately it cleared before the [train] reached the top of the mountain behind Wilkesbarre, and we had a most beautiful view of the valley under that flickering sunlight effect that rain-clouds shadows flitting here and there can make so singularly beautiful. . . . The mountains rolling back and back into the air, the softly gliding river and the sunny skies, I can never forget—would that I had the power to paint them."[12]

The following August, Richards made his first trip to New York City, where he visited the 1853 Exhibition of the Industry of All Nations. Afterward he continued his journey north on the Hudson River. The estuary's alternative designation as the North River emphasized that the broad channel of some three hundred miles was indeed the route into the northern wilderness. For Richards and his generation, as for Cole and Durand before them, this primal New York landscape experience began almost immediately after departure via railroad or steamship from New York City at the river's mouth. Flowing from a source in the high peaks of the Adirondacks along the series of narrow mountain valleys that form its course to the Atlantic, the Hudson River is still portal to many of the sacred sites of American landscape.

Richards traveled some one hundred miles north to visit just such hallowed grounds. Once again, his letters demonstrate how primed he was for seminal landscape encounters. The mountainous formations along the river elicited strong emotional and visual responses: the "mighty rock walls of the Palisades," the Highlands, and West Point. His anticipation of the Catskill Mountains themselves is captured in a description of the distant range as a "majestic outline of the hazy mountains like some noble harmony." He lingered at Catskill village for a day or so to sketch and to pay his respects to the memory of Cole, then dead only five years. Richards acknowledged Cole's primary role

lifelong preoccupation with images of the earth's actual structure would continue to find powerful expression in his dramatic depictions of North American and British coastal topography.

*1853, Gateway to the Adirondacks: The Hudson River Valley*
Richards's August 1852 expedition to Pennsylvania's broad Susquehanna River plain in the Wyoming Valley offered what may well have

as interpreter of the region, noting: "There are pictures upon the walls of the study where he once painted that place at once landscape Art among the foremost of the means of teaching and elevating human nature."[13] The exhibition maintained in the studio included Cole's last series, unfinished at the time his death, a cycle of large paintings called *The Cross and the World*, that featured mountain imagery as powerful visual metaphors in another recapitulation of Bunyan's allegory.

Thus inspired, Richards continued on his way west for a solitary tramp into the Catskill Mountain haunts of the Hudson River School. He spent a week sketching among the dramatic rock walls and waterways in the deep postglacial ravine forming Kaaterskill Clove and Kaaterskill Falls near the spectacular site of the Catskill Mountain House on nearby South Mountain. Letters indicate that Richards interpreted this trip as a turning point. Inspired by his "pilgrimage to the home and grave of Cole" and by his recent study of *The Cross and the World*, he once again enlisted the Bunyanesque metaphor for his own life's course: "And now my sketching trip is over, tomorrow will again see me, a [draftsman]. . . . It seems now as though I had really attained the point from which to work upward, hereby my path has been over what may be likened to the uneven ground that leads us to the foot of a mountain, now have I reached the base, now I begin to ascend."[14] Within six months, he had launched his career, giving up full-time work as a draftsman and joining fellow artist and future Adirondack companion Alexander Lawrie (1828–1917) in a studio on Chestnut Street in Philadelphia.[15]

In constructing his identity as an American artist, Richards had been nurtured by a rich local culture that included the school and galleries of the Pennsylvania Academy of the Fine Arts and the exhibitions of the Art Union of Philadelphia. The city was also home to important private collections and a notable community of artists that included his mentor Paul Weber.[16] Nevertheless, as a young landscape artist in the 1850s, Richards looked to New York City as the center of landscape innovation and production. His professed idols were the luminaries of the New York School: Cole, Church, John Frederick Kensett (1816–1872), and Cropsey. Richards entered what he termed the "race" for fame at a moment dominated by the New York School. Both worshipful and competitive, he tellingly described himself in orbit around these "landscape suns," much of whose fame rested on images of a national landscape type based on sites in New York State and New England.[17]

*1855, The First Adirondack Campaign: Mountain Readiness*

We can imagine Richards's eager anticipation when he had the opportunity in June 1855 to venture into the Adirondack wilderness. This excitement was enhanced by the fact that the journey was an immediate prelude to European travel. Local subscribers in Philadelphia had raised funds to send Richards and Lawrie abroad to complete their artistic education in Paris, Florence, and Düsseldorf. As a preliminary to foreign travel, Richards toured the New York State wilderness for over a month, traveling the length of the Hudson and pressing north to Lake George, Lake Champlain, and into Essex County (fig. 4). On the eve of his departure for a long sojourn abroad, he felt, as Cole had in 1829, the need to "take a 'last, lingering look' at our wild scenery,"[18] scenery that he documented in a series of careful pencil studies (cat. nos. 1–10). The oil paintings produced from these Adirondack sketches after his return from Europe would secure Richards's position as a rising interpreter of those resonant New York sites that constituted a national landscape.

Over a dozen sheets and several pages in a pocket sketchbook document Richards's five-week-long expedition in 1855 from June 20, when he sketched at Fishkill, to July 29, the last view dated in Pleasant Valley. His itinerary took him up the Hudson River to Lake George and Lake Champlain with a stop at historic Fort Ticonderoga on June 29 before continuing west to Pleasant Valley and Elizabethtown for a month, during which he ranged over the valley; the plains of North Elba; the Indian Pass, near the Hudson's source; and the Schroon River, one of its tributaries. These studies are meticulous pencil drawings carefully inscribed with site names and dates, constituting a vivid travel diary and an invaluable documentary record. Because one sketchbook contains both Adirondack and Italian subjects, it is tempting to speculate that Richards took these drawings to Europe.[19] Whether his physical baggage included this corpus of American images or not, it is clear that he carried them in his mind. We know that Richards saw the Adirondack tour as a prologue to European mountain experiences. From Florence he would write to Mitchell of his constant exercises in comparing North America to the mountain landscapes of other nations: "To everyone is not vouchsafed within a few months, a pedestrian excursion through the remote Adirondack mountains—a tramp through part of Switzerland, and a sketching trip for views afoot in the purple passes of the Apennines."[20] Not only was his national scenic allegiance intact—"neither Tuscany or Switzerland has in any way lessened my love of American scenery"—but Richards also concluded that no European landscape artist was equal to New York's Frederic Church.[21]

### 1857/1858, "Our Own Mountains"

Richards married the aspiring poet Anna Matlack (1835–1900) immediately on his return to Philadelphia in June 1856. A honeymoon sketch sojourn in the Wyoming Valley was followed by an excursion to Niagara Falls. European subjects, undertaken to fulfill the commissions that had supported his stay abroad, figured prominently among work undertaken at this time. His mastery of the Northern European mountain manner taught at Düsseldorf, as well as his interest in geology, is evident in an alpine subject like *Rosenlaui Valley and the Wetterhorn*, 1858 (see fig. 3). The marked advance in his technical prowess evident in this dramatic painting had already been duly noted in the press. "[W]e welcome Mr. William T. Richards, the well known Landscape Painter, after his absence on the Continent. Few have returned with greater increase of knowledge, or more admirable landscape material. His studies cannot fail to have decided influence upon his future works, and we confidently anticipate the success of which he had given promise."[22] The annual of the Pennsylvania Academy in the spring of 1857 included both European and American subjects by him.

Richards must have revisited the 1855 New York State sketches as well because the Academy roster also included *Lake George, opposite Caldwell* (cat. no. 14), suggesting his eagerness to rekindle firsthand acquaintance with national sites: "I am anxious to get into the country," he reported to Lawrie who was still abroad, "and study our own mountains. I think we can raise some pretty strong forms—I don't know if my feeling is right—but I like mountains to be cut into ravines and have jumping off precipices [as] well as foliage. I don't thoroughly enjoy a rounded mass of green."[23] The summer of 1857 found Richards once again on the Hudson River. From the village of Coldspring, Richards recounted his excitement at having seen a photograph of Church's monumental painting *Niagara* (Corcoran Gallery of Art, Washington, D.C.) in New York City, including a sketch of the composition in his letter. However, most of the letter is devoted to exaltation at the prospect of three weeks of sketching in and around Coldspring, northern gateway to the Hudson Highlands near West Point. "You must sometime come to this country," he wrote to his wife. "You have not [yet] seen mountains or real rocks. . . ." Richards described Crow's Nest, a peak of some 1,400 feet rising on the west bank next to Storm King, in terms that suggest the kind of mountain experience he sought. Calling it a "splendid subject for a picture," he continued: "Immediately opposite this place rises the strongest and highest of the Highlands—Cronest. The form is very solid and huge—with real grandeur in its simple lines . . . a strong sharp precipiced shape guarding the gorge—I saw this with the red glow of a cloudy sunset behind it . . . but it was strong and apart in its massive quiet—it seemed sentient—folding in its own quiet secrets."[24]

### The Adirondack Oil Paintings: A Landscape Laboratory

By the fall of 1857, fresh from his Coldspring expedition, he began to add American mountain subjects to his repertoire, reporting to Lawrie: "This summer I have been in a better school than Düsseldorf. . . . Lately I have painted only mountains. Intend to master some things in them. . . ."[25] Richards brought to bear a range of empirical experience that now included passages through the Swiss and Italian Alps, the Apennines, and the Rhine valley. These European mountain expeditions intervened between the campaign of sketches made on his initial Adirondack foray and the series of oil paintings shown at the Pennsylvania Academy of the Fine Arts in the spring of 1858. We must assume that, in addition to the recent drawings of the Hudson Highlands, he also consulted his Adirondack drawings of 1855 to produce an all–New York State roster at the Academy that signaled his intention to reestablish his American credentials.[26] These meticulously annotated drawings undoubtedly informed the series of oil paintings. Nevertheless, the compelling topographical accuracy of these on-site documents was not necessarily directly imposed on the pictures composed later in Richards's Philadelphia studio. In the oil paintings, Richards assimilated the elements of his Adirondack scenery according to the visual strategies of the mainstream Hudson River School as he positioned himself to contribute to the canon of a national landscape.[27]

*Lake George: Gateway to the Adirondacks*
Richards's single known painting of Lake George, the most popular site in the region, was exhibited at the Pennsylvania Academy of the Fine Arts in 1857 (cat. no. 14). The subject was a logical one to include as a prelude to his 1858 New York medley because the great lake, some thirty-six miles long and four miles wide, was not only a major tourist destination but also a primary route for the more adventurous into the Adirondack region. A comparison of *Lake George, opposite Caldwell* to three drawings Richards made in the area between June 24 and 26, 1855, is instructive. One drawing of the lake, glimpsed through a foreground screen of trees, suppresses geology for a charming exercise in the picturesque (cat. no. 1), while two other panoramic vistas emphasize the geologically controlled topography (cat. nos. 2, 3). The latter express the glacial structure of the lake basin cupped by austere mountain peaks, a sketching experience that would soon be

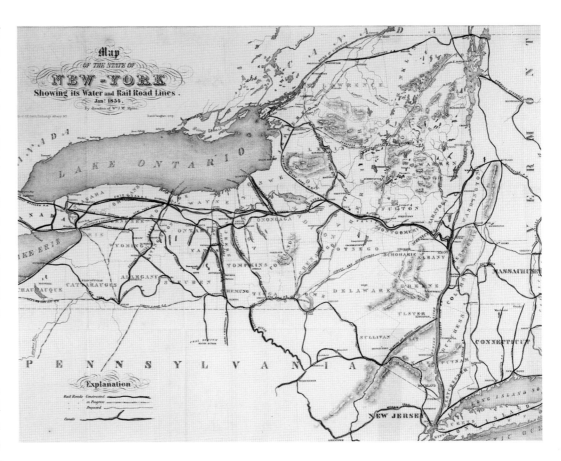

Fig. 4. *Map of the State of New-York showing its Water and Rail Road Lines*, January 1854
J. E. Gavit. Lithograph. The Adirondack Museum

recapitulated on a grander scale in the Alps at Lakes Lucerne and Maggiore.

Richards opted for the domesticated picturesque in his painting, conceiving an image that depicts a rolling but accessible foreground and distant lake under a brilliant sky, a pastoral vignette complete with fisherman and grazing cattle. A wedge of the lake completes the composition in the middle ground, while the mountains beyond operate as our only hint of the great size of this body of water.

19

Fig. 5. *In the Adirondack Mountains*, 1857
William T. Richards (1833–1905). Oil on canvas 30 1/2 x 39 1/2
The St. Louis Art Museum. Bequest of Mr. Albert Blair

*Mountain Majesty: The Solitary Wilderness*
The accomplished exercise of Richards's *In the Adirondack Mountains*, 1857, exhibited at the Pennsylvania Academy in 1858, amply demonstrates his complete command of the panoptic strategies and subject matter associated with the mainstream New York School (fig. 5). Although its precise topographical identity has not been determined, the panoramic sweep of *In the Adirondack Mountains*, the dramatic silhouette of the dying tree against the distant peak, the plunging cataract over whose gorge hovers a rainbow (a tribute, perhaps, to Church's *Niagara*), are all in the tradition of the American wilderness landscape. In this vista, we can locate the artist's emotional response to the subject embodied in elements that, while grounded in natural fact, convey

religious, poetic, and patriotic meaning.

The essence of the picture's national meaning is to be found in the American eagle, set against the rainbow's arch, poised for flight. This close visual association of a biblical symbol and the national emblem of the United States would have been interpreted by a contemporary audience in the era of Manifest Destiny as confirmation of divine purpose active in the New World. *In the Adirondack Mountains* shows an awareness of Church's depictions of vast mountainous regions. Although Church did not paint the Adirondack ranges, there was ample reason for Richards to have had the New York artist-celebrity on his mind as a model. In 1857 Church was famous, not only for *Niagara*, but also for his splendid vision of South America, *The Andes of Ecuador*, 1855 (Reynolda House, Winston-Salem, N.C.), exhibited that spring (1857) at the National Academy of Design, in New York City. In a single year, Church had captivated the public with his interpretations of regions of both North and South America as natural history or, as David Huntington has aptly termed it, "earthscape."[28]

Richards carefully portrayed the wrinkled, eroded, and fissured face of the earth with an insistence on geologic accuracy that owes something to Church as well his study in Düsseldorf, his knowledge of Ruskin, and his own interest in geology. His careful visual exploration of the underlying structure of the rock strata must have been part of the work's appeal to Professor Joseph Leidy, who lent the painting to the Pennsylvania Academy in 1858. Leidy (1823–1891) was an eminent paleontologist at the University of Pennsylvania whose patronage suggests that Richards's image had visual and intellectual appeal in scientific as well as artistic circles. Leidy's research on the rich fossil finds sent back from the western surveys had extended the geologic adventure from efforts to understand the earth's age and origins to include the challenging discovery of extinct life forms as well.

Close in date to this key work is a brilliant view of New York mountain wilderness timbered with first-growth forest in the full glory of a

North American autumn: *Autumn in the Adirondacks*, of 1857–58 (cat. no. 13). This panoramic vista is cloaked in the blazing foliage of fall, creating a rich and varied color effect. In keeping with the chromatic excitement of the picture, brushwork is brisk and energetic. Although we have no record of a fall visit, Richards had many visual and literary models for autumnal imagery. Cole's Adirondack masterwork, *Schroon Mountain*, 1838 (The Cleveland Museum of Art), provides pictorial precedent, and once again his "Essay on American Scenery" offers appropriate language. "There is one season when the American forest surpasses all the world in gorgeousness," Cole had written: "that is the autumnal;—then every hill and dale is riant in the luxury of color. . . . The artist looks despairingly upon the glowing landscape, and in the old world his truest imitation of the American forest at this season are called falsely bright, and scenes in Fairy Land."29 *Autumn in the Adirondacks*, with its heavy mantle of deciduous forest in every phase of the life cycle, offers a virtual exegesis of Cole's characterization of the American autumn. Following Cole's lead, Cropsey developed the autumn season as a particular specialty in the 1850s. Cropsey's autumn landscapes drew on what was by midcentury a distinctively American conception of the chromatic brilliance of the season as absolutely unique to the New World.30 His tacit understanding of this concept is demonstrated by a set of seasons painted in 1860 in which a quartet of nations embodied the four times of year: Switzerland as winter; England as spring; Italy as summer; and the United States as autumn (former collection of Mr. and Mrs. Samuel B. Feld).

However, stimulated by his own plein-air study and by his subject, Richards departs from Cole's golden tones and even the ruddy intensity of Cropsey to work in a palette of extraordinarily high key, one that is nowhere duplicated in his other autumn subjects. His response to the season is echoed in William James Stillman's (1828–1901) letter of September 1859 to *The Crayon* written from the Adirondacks, in which he describes the onset of autumn in the mountain forest as "the carnival of Nature." He outlines the chromatic challenge of such scenery in terms of the new parlance, grounded in science and optics, rather than in the traditional vocabulary of aesthetics.31

*A Pleasant Valley: The Domesticated Wilderness*

In contrast to the wilderness subjects discussed above, another pair of accomplished Adirondack landscapes of the same date (cat. nos. 11, 12) presents a different mountain terrain in which Richards again demonstrated his command of the visual strategies and subject matter associated with the mainstream New York School. Both depict a vista looking west across a halcyon Pleasant Valley with the distinctive double peaks of Cobble Hill and West Cobble dominating the middle distance above Elizabethtown. Giant Mountain rises at the far left and Keene Pass is visible to the right of West Cobble with the profile of Hurricane Mountain seen in the far right distance. A body of water in the foreground represents the Bouquet River, widened here to lake status, controlled by a green, partially cultivated land dotted with evidence of human habitation. Richards has turned the valley floor into a domesticated wilderness environment, even including in *A View in the Adirondacks* a distant but meticulously realized harvest scene. He celebrates Elizabethtown as a bucolic hamlet-haven in Pleasant Valley; as a place name conferred by early settlers, it must have carried irresistible associations for the artist with the descriptive place names in the symbolic topography of Bunyan's allegory.32 The view was easily recognizable because of Cobble's twin peaks and would reappear in drawings and paintings of the 1860s.

The same careful sketch of July 29, 1855 (cat. no. 10), evidently served Richards for *A View in the Adirondacks* (cat. no. 12) and *In the Adirondacks* (cat. no. 11). Both paintings follow the drawing with care in recording the alternately wooded and bare face of Cobble's peaks as well as the topographical profile of the more distant mountain ranges. However, both paintings place less emphasis on the open-ended panoramic vista of the drawing, dwelling instead on similar but not identical foregrounds that are studio inventions of cultivated landscapes with a mill, house, and boats. Each foreground also features a lakelike body of water as an effective compositional device that mirrors the sky. Although the drawing observes a general disposition of light and shadow, there is no sense of the very specific atmospheric conditions demonstrated in the oil paintings. As exercises in landscape com-

Fig. 6. *Study on Upper Saranac Lake, Adirondack Mountains*, 1854
William James Stillman (1828–1901). Oil on canvas 30 1/2 x 25 1/2
Museum of Fine Arts, Boston. Gift of Dr. J. Sydney Stillman, 1977.842

position, *In the Adirondacks* and *A View in the Adirondacks* present the same view under different conditions, as if Richards had set himself the pedagogical task of rendering contrasting effects of weather, atmosphere, and light.

*In the Adirondacks* may be the painting called *Morning in the Adirondac Mountains* that was singled out for its "conspicuous merit" when

exhibited at the Washington Art Association in 1858.[33] A warm aerial glow suggesting a time around sunrise illuminates the mountaintop, reflected in the still mirror surface of the foreground waters in a unifying atmospheric radiance. *A View in the Adirondacks* is a picture of almost the same size and surely painted at the same time. In this work, a cloudy turbulent sky casts a dappled pattern of clear, cold light and shadow over the landscape, in contrast to the more evenly diffused light of the former picture, where the mountain peak and view in general are enveloped in a softening veil of warm atmospheric color-light. The body of water echoes this atmospheric restlessness, its surface slightly disturbed, breaking reflections into areas of light and dark without the clear object definition found on the still water in the other version.

Durand had encouraged just such attention to atmosphere in Letter V: "I can do little more than urge on you the constant study of [atmosphere's] magic power, daily and hourly, in all its changes, at times shortening, at others lengthening the space before you; now permitting to be defined, in all its ruggedness, the precipice on the mountain side—and now transforming it to a fairy palace, and the solid mountain itself to a film of opal."[34] Both topographic accuracy and poetic license inform the paintings of the first Adirondack campaign. Each composition also deftly incorporates forms of homage to the landscape visions of Richards's New York artist-heroes: Cole, Church, and Cropsey. By such means, Richards could lay claim for himself to a role in the campaign to define a national landscape.

*Tension and Transition: Landscape Rebellion and Civil War*
Despite this early mastery, Richards's moment of wholehearted participation in the larger agenda would be brief. The mounting sectional tensions of the 1850s had already begun to undermine assumptions of widespread political and cultural unity implied in such landscape imagery. While we know little firsthand about Richards's early politics, we do know that chief among the fund-raisers for his European trip was the Unitarian minister William Henry Furness (1802–1896), one of Philadelphia's most outspoken abolitionists. The master engraver

and publisher John Sartain (1808–1897), another of Richards's early supporters, shared Furness's strong antislavery views.[35] The reverend's son, William Henry Jr. (1827–1867), was a fellow artist who joined Richards in Europe and would later paint a portrait of Richards's Quaker wife.[36] Returning to Philadelphia in June 1856, just before their marriage, Richards articulated his own perceptions in a letter to Lawrie: "The country is in a very bad state. There is an important crisis approaching. God only knows what will follow. I have little sympathy with politics however."[37] Nevertheless, Richards did respond as an artist to these social and political tensions in subtle but profound ways over the next decade and beyond, by his choice of landscape subjects and styles. His early course as interpreter of the national landscape would be irrevocably altered by these changes in the cultural environment.

Once again, Richards's Adirondack experience would figure prominently in this passage. He returned almost every summer to work in the region from 1862 to 1868. Extant drawings, located paintings, and the titles of others indicate the continuing primacy for him of Essex County, especially Elizabethtown and Keene Valley. He was not alone. Letters, diaries, and the periodical press recorded the summertime artist excursions in the region. Lawrie, Richards's studiomate and companion in Europe, recorded meeting him at Elizabethtown in 1863, 1865, and in 1868. The hamlet was a kind of crossroads for artists. While Lawrie and Richards were there in 1863, Sanford R. Gifford (1823–1880), Jervis McEntee (1828–1891), and Richard W. Hubbard (1816–1888) all passed through. In August 1865 Lawrie and his party returned there from an eight-day camp on the Upper and Lower Ausable Lakes. The group included Richards and his former students Fidelia Bridges (1835–1923) and Arthur Parton

Fig. 7. From *Photographic Studies by W. J. Stillman*
*Part I. The Forest. Adirondac Woods*
William J. Stillman (1828–1901)
The Adirondack Museum P 30523

(1842–1914) as well as Homer Dodge Martin (1836–1897) and his wife. Such excursions and meetings must have been the occasion for comparison of sketches and exchange of ideas. The careful detail of Lawrie's own *Village, Essex County, New York*, of about 1867 (cat. no. 55), suggests that he was influenced by Richards's own meticulous approach. We know the two sketched and painted out-of-doors together on more than one occasion.[38]

### A Landscape of Reconciliation

What was the meaning of the landscape experience that annually drew Richards and his fellows to this rugged terrain during and immediately after the turbulent years of the Civil War? Like Albert Bierstadt's (1830–1902) travels to the Far West, we can theorize that the Adirondack wilderness represented for these artists and their audience a vision of nature unspoiled, a promise of national renewal made even more urgent when weighed against the grim realities of the war.[39] Barely a year after the career-defining Adirondack painting series of 1857–58, Richards began to retreat from single-minded pursuit of a national program of panoramic wilderness subjects by espousing Ruskin's Pre-Raphaelite program of prolonged and laborious study from nature. The English critic's *Modern Painters*, a series of five influential books (1843–60), argued for a new approach to landscape painting that replaced traditional old master models with keen on-site observation and strenuous plein-air study. On the home front, the magazine *The Crayon* also endorsed Ruskin's landscape reform even while publishing Durand's "Letters on Landscape," which also mandated a regimen of plein-air study.[40]

The Adirondacks had already figured in the American Ruskinian development. Stillman, student of Church, co-editor with Durand's son

Fig. 8. *And Some Fell among Thorns*, ca. 1863. William T. Richards (1833–1905) Oil on canvas measurements unknown. Location unknown

John of *The Crayon*, and Ruskin's earliest American artist-disciple, had conducted his own Pre-Raphaelite landscape painting experiments in the Adirondacks, evidenced in the meticulous, even obsessive, finish of his *Study on Upper Saranac Lake, Adirondack Mountains*, 1854 (fig. 6). Stillman returned to the Adirondacks every summer through 1859. His final production, *The Philosopher's Camp*, 1858 (Concord Free Library, Mass.), commemorated the famous 1858 expedition of Cambridge friends, including two of Richards's heroes, Ralph Waldo Emerson and Louis Agassiz, to Follensby Pond. Ultimately despairing of his manual capacity to capture specifics, Stillman abandoned painting to embrace photography in a continuing effort to record every detail of the Adirondack forest. His seminal work, *The Adirondack Portfolio* of 1859, acknowledged as one of the pioneering efforts in American photography, was conceived and executed in the spirit of Ruskinian landscape study.[41] The eye of the camera lens replaced that of the artist in a selfless record of the forest interior (fig. 7).

Richards, a member of the next generation of American Pre-Raphaelites, would persist in his art and by 1861, when Stillman retired from the field, had become the best-known landscape painter among Ruskin's disciples in the United States. Richards was elected to the Pre-Raphaelites' short-lived Association for the Advancement of Truth in Art. The association's artist members rejected Cole's American landscapes as models, focusing instead on laboriously detailed, brilliantly colored landscapes and still lifes often painted out-of-doors.[42] Richards's Ruskinian regimen led to his producing landscapes that are all foreground, informed by a claustrophobic vision set at ground level and limited to objects immediately before the eye with little or no recession (fig. 8).

These marvels of close study, painted during the years of the Civil War, were also dense allegories of horticultural and agricultural symbolism. Their botanical protagonists enacted a series of narratives inspired by the Parable of the Sower from the Gospel of Matthew, a biblical source that had been used by the English Pre-Raphaelites. Paintings with titles like *And Some Fell among Thorns* (fig. 8) and *Neglected Corner of a Wheatfield*, 1865 (private collection), may be read as moral allegories of the contrast between good and poor husbandry. Unruly weeds threaten to invade the orderly rows of grain. These narratives could not fail to be read as national and political by an American audience in 1863 and 1865, when the Union cause was often symbolized in the popular press by wheat (and the Confederate by cotton plants).[43]

The complex allegories encoded within these paintings would also emerge in a unique Adirondack subject: *John Brown's Grave (Sketch)*, of about 1864 (cat. no. 26), one of the few titles in Richards's oeuvre to reflect the impact of politics and current events. The little painting depicts the recently executed abolitionist's memorial plot on his farm at North Elba. Brown's dramatic career and tragic end (he was hanged in December 1859) provided subjects for few paintings. The most famous is Thomas Hovenden's (1840–1895) *The Last Moments of John Brown*, 1884 (The Metropolitan Museum of Art, New York), painted long after the fact.[44] Richards's contemporaneous response to the subject is oblique and coded in both landscape and harvest imagery, rather than the figural narrative of history painting. During the Civil War and the years immediately following, the harvest field seen pressing up to the martyr's gravesite was also invested with another set of diverse meanings. A number of American paintings in the 1860s, including George Inness's (1824–1894) *Peace and Plenty*, 1865, and Winslow Homer's (1836–1910) *The Veteran in a New Field*, 1865 (both, The Metropolitan Museum of Art, New York), enlisted harvest themes to express themes of loss and reconciliation associated with the Civil War era.[45]

In the 1850s, when Richards came of age as a landscape painter, the harvest image had already been embraced as a national theme. Durand interpreted both the mountain wilderness and harvest as an allegory of progress in *The First Harvest in the Wilderness*, 1855 (fig. 9), combining visual memories of the Adirondack and White Mountains to create his remote mountain farm location. A pioneer farmer (representing Augustus Graham, a recently deceased Brooklyn philanthropist) gathers his first crop from a field cleared only a short time before. In a fascinating parallel of art and life, the memorial and commemorative meaning of the painting is visualized in the erratic boulder poised at the edge of the imaginary homestead, inscribed with Graham's name. Four years later, Brown would leave instructions to co-opt the great glacial boulder on his farm at North Elba as a colossal headstone to mark his grave, perhaps sensing that it would come to serve as a monument to his cause as well (fig. 10).

Richards's fascinating little painting enlists the harvest theme in multivalent readings that place this work very much in the context of the parable images. Tombstone and plow reference the Grim Reaper, while the grainfield, a sapling, and a faint rainbow suggest rebirth, blending martyrdom, memory, and hope. These images also embodied the motto of "John Brown's Body Lies A 'Mouldering in the Grave," a popular marching song that quickly became the unofficial anthem of Union troops. This poignant foreground motif is set against a distant view of the high peaks, anchoring us to the specific Adirondack site and, perhaps, reenacting on a distant but hopeful note an emblem of national unity in what I have suggested might be termed a landscape of reconciliation.

The juxtaposition of moment, monument, and mountain in *John Brown's Grave (Sketch)* leads us to speculate about whether this Adirondack site of antebellum antislavery activity, made famous by Brown's violent abolitionist campaigns in Kansas and Virginia, as well as their after-

Fig. 9. *The First Harvest in the Wilderness*, 1855
Asher B. Durand (1796–1886). Oil on canvas 32 1/8 x 48 1/16
Brooklyn Museum of Art, New York

math in the Civil War, led to a general association of the region with the Union cause.[46] The painting belonged to the dealer and collector Samuel P. Avery, who lent it for exhibition at the Brooklyn Art Association in May 1864 at the height of Sanitary Fair activity to raise funds in major cities of the Union. Works by Richards were displayed at the Brooklyn Long Island Sanitary Fair in March, and he participated in New York City's Metropolitan Fair in April. Richards was also active in plans for the Philadelphia fair, and it is worth noting that Adirondack subjects figured among his works displayed in the Great Central Fair held that June in Philadelphia.[47] These included Professor Leidy's *In the Adirondack Mountains*, 1857 (see fig. 5), and a charming fantasy on an Adirondack theme, *A Valley in the Adirondacks*, of about 1864

Fig. 10. *John Brown's Grave at North Elba*, ca. 1880. Seneca Ray Stoddard (1843–1917). Photograph. The Adirondack Museum P 1467

(cat. no. 27). This small oil painting casts Pleasant or Keene Valley as a Turnersque vision of truly delectable mountains. Richards depicts an earthly paradise of wooded peaks and valleys conceived in pastel hues and emerging from a distance suffused in golden light and luminous vapors. Tiny figures at rest in the elevated foreground humanize this hospitable wilderness of sunlit plains, shining lakes, and meandering rivers, completing the Arcadian vision redolent of the English master's pastoral landscapes and underscoring the elegiac mood appropriate for the occasion of its commission. The latter was originally bound with other works in a handsome album: *Sketches by Philadelphia, New York and Boston Artists* (cat. no. 28). This collaborative effort "containing contributions from our best men" was presented to the famed actress Charlotte Cushman to honor her fund-raising efforts on behalf of the United States Sanitary Commission.[48]

Richards's patronage offers another intriguing clue to the possibility of wider connotations for Adirondack scenery. It is interesting to note that Robert Stafford Hale (1822–1881), a prominent Elizabethtown attorney and elected official as well as a friend with whom Richards may have lodged, owned not only the impressive 1864 view of Elizabeth-

town and Pleasant Valley from Woods Hill (cat. no. 24) but also an engraving after one of Richards's Pre-Raphaelite parable paintings, *And Some Fell among Thorns* (see fig. 8).[49] This matrix of clues and coincidence leads us to speculate on what larger meanings beyond topographical record might be encoded within the more straightforward views of Pleasant and Keene Valleys discussed below (cat. nos. 24, 25, 29, 30; fig. 11). Richards exhibited these handsome panoramas to generally favorable critical review between 1863 and 1866. At the same time, however, the artist also took considerable critical heat for such Pre-Raphaelite exercises as *And Some Fell among Thorns*. Reviewers universally admired the latter as technical tours de force of botanical accuracy. Henry T. Tuckerman, for example, referred to them as "miracles of special study."[50] Nevertheless, these works were also taken to task, often harshly, as literal, mimetic, and unimaginative. Richards's Pre-Raphaelite paintings became a lightning rod for positive and negative opinion during the brief heyday of the American movement.

## "His Two Moods"

In contrast, Richards's contemporaneous Adirondack subjects seemed to offer an opportunity to reconcile the atmospheric requirements of landscape painting and the Pre-Raphaelite demand for detail. Like the works of the 1850s, the oil paintings of the second campaign are grounded in a group of wonderful drawings charting itinerary as well as response when he returned to the area in 1862 (cat. no. 15) and, again, for a well-documented stay in 1863 that included a marvelous sketchbook (cat. nos. 16–19). Like the drawings of the 1855 campaign, these are an independent body of work, never exhibited in the artist's lifetime but held in his studio. Worthy of note on aesthetic and documentary terms, they constitute both a visual diary and an artist's itinerary. They are compelling records of experience in a region many of whose landmarks are still intact. A few open-air studies executed in oil on paper also survive (cat. nos. 21–23). In his diary, Lawrie recorded painting out-of-doors with Richards during a nine-week period in 1863. Probably representative of a larger corpus of plein-air work now lost, they are brilliant in palette and informal in composition. These little records offer an even more vivid transcript of the hills and meadows surrounding the hamlet of Elizabethtown as they appeared in the early 1860s.

While we now appreciate these on-site records very much for themselves, all of these works served a primary function as studies and reference points for the oil paintings Richards composed from them, which he executed later in the studio. The single exception is the drawing *Indian Pass, Adirondacks,* 1866 (cat. no. 20), which belongs to the interesting category of oversize elaborate exhibition drawings in graphite and charcoal produced between 1864 and 1867. Some of these, like *Indian Pass,* were reproduced as photographs and some are directly related to oil paintings of similar scale. Richards referred to them as "cartoons," suggesting that these works on paper were conceived as full-scale studies that might be executed as oil paintings on commission.[51]

*Indian Pass* is also an exception to the body of known Adirondack images in its exercise of the vertical sublime. The massive boulders, the looming tower of Wallface Mountain, low clouds, and soaring eagles strike a note of gloomy grandeur. This is in contrast to the dominant mood in the landscape paintings, which is one of celebration of the mountain valley pastoral that harks back to the pendant paintings of 1857 (cat. nos. 11, 12). Once again Elizabethtown and the broad plain of Pleasant Valley drew Richards with their appealing blend of comfortable inhabited foreground and middle distance in combination with the distant, austere mountain peaks. The Bouquet River, imagined as a lakelike body of water in 1857, assumes its identity in these paintings as a winding watercourse over the valley floor. Richards dispenses with the dark, stagelike foreground platforms used in the views of 1857, adopting an open-ended panoramic format also put to use by Gifford, Homer Martin, Alfred Thompson Bricher (1837–1905), and others in the 1860s (cat. nos. 45, 50, 40).[52]

While based on site drawings, the paintings are compositions that seem to vary in topographical focus. *Adirondack Landscape,* 1864 (cat. no. 24), is a very precise record of the Elizabethtown hamlet seen from Woods Hill. *Autumn in the Adirondacks* portrays Blueberry and Porter mountains in Keene Valley with Mt. Marcy in the background (cat.

Fig. 11. *Bouquet Valley in the Adirondacks*, 1863
William T. Richards (1833–1905)
Oil on canvas 25 x 36. Altman Fine Arts, New York

no. 29). Other paintings, like *Bouquet Valley in the Adirondacks*, of about 1864 (cat. no. 25), and *The Bouquet Valley, Adirondacks*, 1866 (cat. no. 30), are likewise convincingly steeped in the topographical sense of the region, but have so far defied efforts to identify their specific sites.

The twin peaks of Cobble Hill and West Cobble, familiar from the pendant paintings of 1857, were recorded again in a masterly large drawing of the 1860s to anchor a large painting of 1863 (fig. 11). Perhaps this is the work titled *Bouquet Valley in the Adirondacks* that, with a Pre-Raphaelite work called *Landscape*, was exhibited at the Pennsylvania Academy in 1863. These two paintings were compared and discussed at length in *The Round Table* as highly representative of Richards's dualistic approaches to landscape subjects:

*W. T. Richards is represented by two pictures which fairly exhibit his two moods. The first . . . Landscape, . . . is more characteristic, at least*

Fig. 12. *Nantucket*, 1865
William T. Richards (1833–1905)
Oil on canvas 8 x 16
Private collection

*more as we have been accustomed to see in his works . . . rendered with
all fidelity . . . he endeavors to put upon his canvas the works of nature
as he sees them, omitting nothing, generalizing nothing. . . . Mr. Richards's
other picture,* Bouquet Valley in the Adirondacks, *is very different in
conception and execution, but we recognize the same faithful hand carefully transcribing every growth of the foreground, and clothing the distant hills in the gold sunshine of midsummer. Yet this picture does not
altogether satisfy us; there is a thinness in the manner, and a want of large-
ness of style which prevent its taking the highest rank.*[53]

Critics were very well aware of the contrasting modes or "moods"
in which Richards worked, as well as the difficulties in blending
extremes of detail with pictorial coherence and atmospheric breadth.
Tuckerman complained that in Richards's Pre-Raphaelite paintings
"the relative finish of the foreground, centre, and background is not
always harmonious."[54]

## "A Feeling for Air"

In the summer of 1865 Richards divided his time between mountain and shore, spending time in July on the island of Nantucket.
The September issue of *The Round Table* commented on the summer's sketches at both places, noting that some were "general expressions of form and color, rather than the elaborate studies to which
he had usually devoted his time. Some of these sketches appear . . .
to promise something greater than he has yet produced, and I look
forward with great interest for their elaboration into pictures."[55]
In these Nantucket oil sketches, Richards's response to the bright,
clear light of the seashore is recorded with particular success (fig.
12). Their simple composition—sea and shore in a zone below
and the sky above—suggests that the light and realities of topography at the coast moved Richards deeply, and the influence continued to inform his studies after he moved inland. By August
Richards was back in the Adirondacks, joining a party of artists who
enjoyed an eight-day camping expedition on the Upper and Lower
Ausable Lakes in nearby Keene.[56] Returning to Germantown by
September, he assembled his Adirondack sketches and studies to
develop the largest known painting of the series and arguably the masterwork of the 1860s campaign: *The Bouquet Valley, Adirondacks*,
1866 (cat. no. 30).

From an elevated point we gaze far down Pleasant Valley, bordered
by mountains and bathed in a luminous haze of mist and light. The
vista is firmly grounded in observed fact, but still redolent of the tran-
scendent haze in the Charlotte Cushman Album fantasy landscape of
1864 (cat. no. 27). The broad plain winds between wooded slopes in
a slow curve from right to left toward a profile of more distant mountains, probably the rugged high peak district of Keene. Foreground,
middle distance, and background are convincingly presented as a uni-
fied atmospheric whole. After a decade or more of outdoor study and
steady painting, Richards had won his own knowledge of atmosphere
as Durand had written of it in "The Letters": as "the power which
defines and measures space" and the "veil or medium interposed
between the eye and all visible objects. . . . It is *felt* in the foreground,"

Durand had observed, "*seen* beyond that, and *palpable* in the distance."[57] Richards also made deft use of the panoramic canvas format, effectively employed here to suggest the terrain's expanding beyond the physical frame of the picture. The viewer's commanding elevated vantage point also implies an element of human control, even over wilderness spaces like the Adirondacks.

In this masterful landscape painting of 1866, one of his final Adirondack statements, Richards might be said to have at last achieved that balance of breadth and detail demanded by his critics. Another unlocated Adirondack subject of that year bore a suggestive preamble: *Repose*, to its otherwise site-specific title, *Mt. Marcy and Avalanche Lake, among the Adirondacks*. The painting elicited public praise that might well be applied to *The Bouquet Valley, Adirondacks*:

*The atmosphere of the picture can be breathed; the trees, rocks, water, it is difficult to believe could be more faithfully rendered from nature. . . . "Repose" is the language of all portions of the canvas, from the little heather blossom at the foot of the moss-covered rocks to the "solemn, cloud-capped mountain" in the background. Richards has given us his best mark in this picture, and as he now leaves for Europe in the next steamer, he will go with a fresh and enhanced reputation, as the first American artist in his special department, the school of the pre-Raphaelites; and we hope he will lose none of his originality, or distinctive peculiarities by the tour and sojourn in the old world.*[58]

In fact, the Ruskinian radicals had largely disbanded by the time Richards and his family departed for Paris in November. Nevertheless, his reputation as a Pre-Raphaelite endured. This legacy of close attention to descriptive detail earned increasing criticism, especially as American taste in the 1870s began to turn toward an ever more painterly, suggestive approach to landscape. For nearly a decade, Richards had attempted to accommodate critics and patrons by the concurrent practice of dual landscape types, alternating the spatial and meteorological concerns of the mainstream landscape approach with the microscopic detail of the American Pre-Raphaelites. The tensions imposed by

Fig. 13. George Whitney's art gallery in his Philadelphia residence. *The Bouquet Valley, Adirondacks* is hanging to the left of the doorway to the watercolor gallery.
George B. Wood Jr. Photograph, ca. 1885. George Whitney Papers 1885, Archives of American Art, Smithsonian Institution

this kind of stylistic schizophrenia and the persistent criticism of his Pre-Raphaelite extremism must have contributed in the late 1860s to the impulse to experiment with watercolor as a new exhibition medium and to explore a new subject, the American coast. By the time he left for a year in Europe, his summertime travels were divided between the Adirondacks and the New England seashore. His return a year later would mark a continuous shift in subject emphasis from landscape to the coast and sea.

*The Bouquet Valley, Adirondacks* belonged to George Whitney (1820–1885), Richards's major patron, who was a Philadelphia manufacturer of railroad car wheels and an important collector of both American and European paintings. Whitney traveled to Elizabethtown with Richards in 1868 to visit the site of his painting, and, perhaps, the rich iron ore deposits in the region attracted his industrialist interests as well.[59] This excursion, reported in Lawrie's journal, would be Richards's last recorded visit to the region until 1904. The painting itself was displayed in Whitney's private art gallery in Philadel-

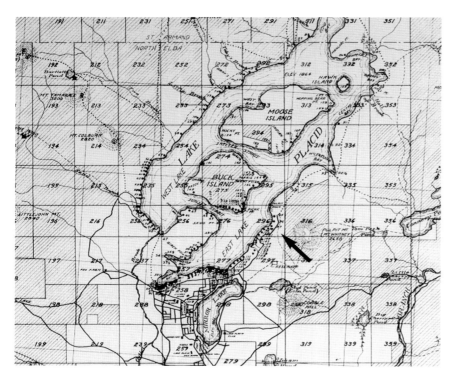

Fig. 14. Map of Lake Placid and vicinity, 1904. Published by the Lake Placid Shore Owners' Association, Lake Placid, New York. Curly Birch Camp is on East Lake, just below Pulpit Rock. The Adirondack Museum Library

phia (fig. 13) until 1885, when the entire collection, including eighty-seven works by Richards, had to be sold at auction after the collector's sudden death. By then Whitney's European and American paintings were considered old-fashioned. The press described Richards's landscapes as "more like geological and botanical studies than like art. . . . None of our clever young landscape painters would so waste effort . . . but how far is this because they know better, and how far because they care less."[60] The knowledge base of Richards's formative years, a reverence for visual facts rendered with great care, had been devalued, replaced by preference for painterly bravura and a general preoccupation with picture-making skills over content.

Richards had long been anxious about becoming an old-fashioned landscape painter. The "time is past," he had confided to Whitney in 1879, "when the American people can hunger for my pictures if they ever did. I feel that I am an old fogy, and can expect little favor in competition with the new men."[61] In response, he had established himself as a respected marine specialist in both oil and the hugely popular watercolor medium. From 1874 he summered regularly in Newport, becoming identified with images of the Rhode Island as well as the New Jersey coast, the subjects for which he is still best known today. A two-year sojourn in England from 1878 to 1880 expanded Richards's domestic market with British coastal subjects. Despite the personal and market calamity of the 1885 Whitney sale, Richards rebounded to maintain an active and productive career for another two decades, primarily as an interpreter of the American coast and sea.

*1904, Lake Placid: The Final Adirondack Campaign*
Nonetheless, Richards never completely abandoned landscape painting. In 1884 his purchase of a farm property in Chester County provided the opportunity for a six-year campaign in the Pennsylvania countryside of regular plein-air study in oils. The Chester County interlude was the catalyst as well for the production of a series of stately landscapes whose painterly surfaces and pastoral mood indicate Richards's participation in an international Barbizon moment.[62] The practice of painting in oils out-of-doors was not new for Richards. We have early evidence in Lawrie's reports of their Adirondack painting expeditions, as well as the several vivid little plein-air notes in oil that survive as records of excursions in and around Elizabethtown (cat. nos. 21–23). However, Richards would systematize his plein-air procedures and methods during the Chester County years, adopting regular sizes for the composition and wooden panels that he carried in paint cases that also served as easels.[63] These cases accompanied him in a springboard wagon over the roads and lanes of the Brandywine region. After the sale of the farm in 1891, he carried them on his frequent trips abroad to England, Ireland, and Scotland; to Italy, Norway, and the Channel Islands; as well as on surveys of his home territory in Rhode Island.

In 1904 he remained stateside, returning to Essex County with plein-air equipment for a summer holiday at Lake Placid in the company of his artist-daughter Anna. Father and daughter recorded their lakeside sojourn in a series of small oil paintings.[64] Their base of operations was Curly Birch Camp, on East Lake near Pulpit Rock opposite Sunset Strait and Buck Island (fig. 14). The cottage (cat. no. 36) had been built by Amanda Brewster Sewell (1859–1926), a local artist of note.[65] Two wonderful photographs show Richards at work, neatly, even formally, attired, seated on a camp stool and sheltered by an umbrella with easel box on his lap. His method of painting from top to bottom is recorded in one over-the-shoulder view taken at water's edge as he captured a view of Whiteface Mountain (frontispiece). Another shows him perched on a rock shelf above the lake amid boulders and forest, gazing outward, sketch box open on his knees (fig. 15).

Fig. 15. *William T. Richards painting at Lake Placid,* 1904
Photograph taken by his daughter Eleanor Richards Price (1862–1954)
Collection of David and Inge Price

On panels measuring almost ten by fifteen inches, Richards undertook a series of oil studies around the perimeter of the lake that form an extraordinary document of time and place. Each painting is consistent in size, approach, and subject, yet subtly distinctive. Most of these images include the unique profile of Whiteface Mountain rising separate and apart from the other High Peaks some seven miles to the northeast. The distant summit, deeply scarred by glaciers and rock slides, is carefully charted in one oil sketch taken right at the water's edge under conditions of unusual climatic clarity (cat. no. 31). Clear skies and sunshine preside over the blue wind-driven lake surface too choppy to offer reflections of the brilliant greens of summer foliage. More typically, however, overcast skies with rain clouds and veils of mist prevail as environment in the Lake Placid studies (cat. nos. 32–34). These conditions subdue the range of colors to a subtle palette of grays, silver, and dark greens that are often reflected, as are the distant mountain ranges, in the still lake water. Richards's touch is painterly and sure, confident in capturing every characteristic of mountain-lake topography as well as each and every nuance of weather and light in these simple, even minimal, compositions whose monumentality belies their small scale. These works celebrate solitary nature: people are absent; even boats are rare. Artist and viewer join in silent contemplation to experience the spiritual renewal made possible in mountain-lake solitude. The Lake Placid oil studies are an exquisite coda as well, a reminder of the abiding landscape passion that had brought a twenty-two-year-old aspiring artist from Philadelphia to the remote northern mountains of New York State half a century before.

1. Information about Richards's biography and career is found in Linda S. Ferber, *William Trost Richards: American Landscape and Marine Painter*, exh. cat. (Brooklyn: The Brooklyn Museum, 1973), hereafter cited as Ferber, *Richards* (1973); Linda S. Ferber, *William Trost Richards (1833–1905): American Landscape and Marine Painter* (New York: Garland Publishing, 1980), hereafter cited as Ferber, *Richards* (1980); Linda S. Ferber, *"Never at Fault": The Drawings of William Trost Richards*, exh. cat. (Yonkers, N.Y.: The Hudson River Museum, 1986), hereafter cited as Ferber, *Richards* (1986).

2. For Paul Weber, see David Patterson McCarthy, "A Great Success: Paul Weber's Career as a Landscape Painter in Philadelphia, 1848–1860," M.A. thesis, University of Delaware, 1988, hereafter cited as McCarthy 1988; for Edward Moran, see Paul D. Schweitzer, *Edward Moran (1829–1901): American Marine and Landscape Painter*, exh. cat. (Wilmington: Delaware Art Museum, 1979); for Haseltine, see Marc Simpson et al., *Expressions of Place: The Art of William Stanley Haseltine*, exh. cat. (San Francisco: The Fine Arts Museums of San Francisco, 1992); for Lewis, see Michael W. Schantz, *Edmund Darch Lewis, 1835–1910*, exh. cat. (Philadelphia: Woodmere Art Museum, 1985).

3. For information about the discourse on mountains and the Sublime, see Walter John Hipple Jr., *The Beautiful, the Sublime and the Picturesque in Eighteenth-Century British Aesthetic Theory* (Carbondale: The Southern Illinois University Press, 1957); and Marjorie Hope Nicholson, *Mountain Gloom and Mountain Glory: The Development of the Aesthetics of the Infinite* (Ithaca, N.Y.: Cornell University Press, 1959).

4. For *The Pilgrim's Progress* as a popular artists' theme, see Ferber, *Richards* (1980), 29–41.

5. William T. Richards to William H. Willcox, Philadelphia, January 18, 1854, roll 2296, William Trost Richards Papers, ca. 1850–1914, Archives of American Art, Smithsonian Institution (hereafter cited as Richards Papers, AAA), quoted in Ferber, *Richards* (1980), 31.

6. Durand opened his final lesson by comparing the course to a challenging but rewarding climb: "If you have ever ascended a high mountain, even by a well-defined path, you must have encountered many difficulties . . . and practically learned, that a short sentence of directions involved miles of toilsome labor, and it is thus with the precepts and practice of Art; especially in the direction I have endeavored to point out. But believing it to be the direct path to the main summit, I could not commend an easier way to a secondary elevation." Asher B. Durand, "Letters on Landscape Painting: Letter IX," *The Crayon*, July 11, 1855, 16.

7. For geology and American landscape painting, see Barbara Novak, *Nature and Culture: American Landscape Painting, 1825–1875* (New York: Oxford University Press, 1980; rev. ed. 1996); Rebecca Bedell, *The Anatomy of Nature: Geology and American Landscape Painting, 1825–1875* (Princeton, N.J.: Princeton University Press, 2001).

8. William T. Richards to James Mitchell, Philadelphia, October 29, 1854, roll 2296, Richards Papers, AAA, quoted in Ferber, *Richards* (1980), 107.

9. For Ruskin's influence in the United States, see Roger B. Stein, *John Ruskin and Aesthetic Thought in America, 1840–1900* (Cambridge, Mass.: Harvard University Press, 1967).

10. N.P.C., "Relation between Geology and Landscape Painting," *The Crayon*, August 1859, 256.

11. For the American Pre-Raphaelite circle, see Ferber, *Richards* (1980), chap. 4, "W. T. Richards as an American Pre-Raphaelite"; and Linda S. Ferber and William H. Gerdts, *The New Path: Ruskin and the American Pre-Raphaelites*, exh. cat. (New York: the Brooklyn Museum and Schocken Books, 1985), hereafter cited as Ferber and Gerdts, *The New Path* (1985).

12. Richards to Mitchell, August 8, 1852, roll 2296, Richards Papers, AAA.

13. Richards to Mitchell, Philadelphia, August 28, 1853, roll 2296, Richards Papers, AAA, quoted in Ferber, *Richards* (1986), 20. For Cole, see Ellwood C. Parry III, *The Art of Thomas Cole: Ambition and Imagination* (Newark: University of Delaware Press, 1988); and William H. Truettner and Alan Wallach, *Thomas Cole: Landscape into History*, exh. cat. (New Haven and London: Yale University Press; Washington, D.C.: National Museum of American Art, Smithsonian Institution, 1994).

14. Richards to Mitchell, Philadelphia, August 28, 1853, roll 2296, Richards Papers, AAA.

15. For Lawrie, see Peggy O'Brien, "Alexander Lawrie, 1828–1917: Adirondack Artist," *Adirondac*, May 1984, 24–29; and Mary Ann Goley and Robin Pell, *Alexander Lawrie: Views of Essex County, New York*, exh. cat. (Washington, D.C.: Federal Reserve Board Fine Arts Program, 1993), hereafter cited as *Lawrie*, 1993.

16. For Philadelphia's cultural life and collections, see Katherine Martinez and Page Talbott, eds., *Philadelphia's Cultural Landscape: The Sartain Family Legacy* (Philadelphia: Temple University Press, 2000), hereafter cited as Martinez and Talbott 2000; E[arl] S[hinn], "Private Art-Collections of Philadelphia," *Lippincott's Magazine* 9 (April–June 1872), 10 (July–December 1872).

17. Richards to Mitchell, Philadelphia, April 27, 1854, roll 2296, Richards Papers, AAA, quoted in Ferber, *Richards* (1980), 19.

18. Thomas Cole to Robert Gilmor, New York, April 26, 1829, quoted in Howard S. Merritt, "A Wild Scene: Genesis of a Painting," *The Baltimore Museum of Art Annual* 2 (1967): 67.

19. The sketchbook is in the collection of the Brooklyn Museum of Art, Gift of Edith Ballinger Price, 1975.15.2.

20. Richards to Mitchell, Florence, December 7, 1855, roll 2296, Richards Papers, AAA.

21. Ibid.; and Richards to Thomas Webb Richards, Paris, August 29, 1855, typescript in author's collection.

22. *Philadelphia Daily Evening Bulletin*, June 12, 1856, sec. 2, 2. I am indebted to Merl M. Moore Jr. for bringing this and many other references to Richards in the press and periodicals to my attention.

23. Richards to Alexander Lawrie, Philadelphia, April 13, 1857, collecton of David Trout.

24. Richards to Anna M. Richards, Coldspring, New York, [August] 1857, private collection.

25. Richards to Lawrie, Philadelphia, September 13, 1857, collection of David Trout.

26. The New York subjects exhibited at the Academy in 1858 were 129. *Pleasant Valley, Adirondack Mountains.* H. Earl; 154. *View on the Hudson River—Afternoon.* For sale. W. T. Richards; 297. *In the Adirondack Mountains.* Dr. Joseph Leidy; 318. *Crows'-nest (Hudson River).* H. Earl.

27. For the Hudson River School and a national landscape, see John K. Howat et al., *American Paradise: The World of the Hudson River School*, exh. cat. (New York: The Metropolitan Museum of Art and Harry N. Abrams, 1987); Kenneth Myers et al., *The Catskills: Painters, Writers, and Tourists in the Mountains, 1820–1895*, exh. cat. (Yonkers, N.Y.: The Hudson River Museum, 1987); Angela Miller, *The Empire of the Eye: Landscape Representation and American Cultural Politics, 1825–1875* (Ithaca, N.Y.: Cornell University Press, 1993), hereafter cited as Miller, *Empire* (1993).

28. David C. Huntington, *The Landscapes of Frederic Edwin Church: Vision of an American Era* (New York: George Braziller, 1966), xi.

29. Thomas Cole, "Essay" (1835), 106.

30. For Cropsey, see Peter Bermingham, *Jasper F. Cropsey, 1823–1900: A Retrospective of America's Painter of Autumn*, exh. cat. (College Park: University of Maryland Art Gallery, 1968); and William S. Talbot, *Jasper F. Cropsey, 1823–1900,* exh. cat. (Washington, D.C.: The National Collection of Fine Arts, Smithsonian Institution, 1970).

31. W[illiam] J. S[tillman], "Country Correspondence: Adirondac Woods, Sept. 15th," *The Crayon* 6 (October 1859): 321–22.

32. For Essex County, see Winslow C. Watson, *The Military and Civil History of the County of Essex, New York and a General Survey of its Physical Geography, its Mines and Minerals, and Industrial Pursuits* (Albany, N.Y.: J. Munsell, 1869); and H. P. Smith, ed., *History of Essex County* (Syracuse, N.Y.: D. Mason & Co., 1885), hereafter cited as Smith 1885.

33. "Washington Art Association Exhibition," *The Cosmopolitan Art Journal* 2 (1857–58): 140, quoted in Ferber, *Richards* (1980), 113.

34. Durand, "Letter V," March 7, 1855, 146, quoted in Ferber, *Richards* (1980), 114.

35. For Furness, see *Dictionary of American Biography*, ed. Allen Johnson and Dumas Malone (New York: Charles Scribner's Sons, 1946), 7:80; Elizabeth M. Geffen, "William Henry Furness: Philadelphia Anti-Slavery Preacher," *The Pennsylvania Magazine of History and Biography* 82 (July 1958): 259–92; and Martinez and Talbott 2000 passim. For Sartain, see Martinez and Talbott 2000.

36. For Anna Matlack Richards, see Harrison S. Morris, *Masterpieces of the Sea: William T. Richards: A Brief Outline of His Life and Art* (Philadelphia: J. B. Lippincott Company, 1912), 43–46; Allen W. Trelease, "A Happy Romance in Letters from Hannah Whitall Smith," *The Friend* 28 (May 1953): 379–81; and Gordon J. Howard, "A Germantown Painter and His Chemist Son," *Germantown Crier*

48 (fall 1998): 40–59. For William Henry Furness Jr., see Henry T. Tuckerman's obituary entry in *Book of the Artists: American Artist Life* (New York: G. P. Putnam and Son, 1867; reprint, New York: James F. Carr, 1967), 479–82, hereafter cited as Tuckerman 1867.

37. Richards to Lawrie, Philadelphia, June 17, 1856, collection of David Trout.

38. Alexander Lawrie diary, Elizabethtown, New York, September 22, 1863, collection of David Trout, quoted in *Lawrie* 1993, 8.

39. Robert L. McGrath addresses this issue in his essay, "Facing North and East: The Ideology of the Gaze," in *Scenes of Placid Lake*, exh. cat. (Lake Placid, N.Y.: Lake Placid Center for the Arts, 1993), hereafter cited as McGrath, *Lake Placid* (1993).

40. For Ruskin and American plein-air painting, see Linda S. Ferber, " 'Determined Realists': The American Pre-Raphaelites and the Association for the Advancement of Truth in Art," in Ferber and Gerdts, *The New Path* (1985), 11–37. For American plein-air painting in the nineteenth century, see Eleanor Jones Harvey, *The Painted Sketch: American Impressions from Nature, 1830–1880*, exh. cat. (Dallas: Dallas Museum of Art, 1998).

41. For Stillman, see Richard D. Bullock, "William James Stillman: The Early Years," Ph.D. diss., University of Michigan, 1976; Linda S. Ferber, " 'The Clearest Lens': William J. Stillman and American Landscape Painting," in Anne Ehrenkranz et al., *Poetic Localities: Photographs of Adirondacks, Cambridge, Crete, Italy, Athens [by] William J. Stillman,* exh. cat. (New York: Aperture in association with the International Center of Photography, 1988), 91–102.

42. For Richards and the American Pre-Raphaelite movement, see Ferber, *Richards* (1980), chap. 4, "W. T. Richards as an American Pre-Raphaelite"; and Ferber and Gerdts, *The New Path* (1985), passim.

43. On the subject of wheat, the Civil War, and the harvest theme, see T. B. Thorpe, "Wheat and Its Association," *Harper's New Monthly Magazine* 15 (August 1857): 301–13, cited in Christopher Kent Wilson, "Winslow Homer's *The Veteran in a New Field*: A Study of the Harvest Metaphor and Popular Culture," *The American Art Journal* 17 (autumn 1985): 9, hereafter cited as Wilson 1985; and James C. Moore, "The Storm and the Harvest: The Image of Nature in Mid-Nineteenth-Century American Landscape Painting," Ph.D. diss., Indiana University, 1974. See also the discussion of later-nineteenth-century American harvest imagery in Linda S. Ferber, *Pastoral Interlude: William T. Richards in Chester County*, exh. cat. (Chadds Ford, Pa.: The Brandywine River Museum, 2001), hereafter cited as Ferber, *Richards* (2001).

44. In her catalogue entry on Hovenden's painting, Natalie Spassky discusses other interpretations of Brown's saga in *American Paintings in the Metropolitan Museum of Art, Volume II: A Catalogue of Works by Artists Born between 1816 and 1845* (New York: The Metropolitan Museum of Art, 1985), 541–44.

45. See Wilson 1985, passim.

46. McGrath, *Lake Placid* (1993) discusses the association of Lake Placid and Whiteface with the John Brown site in North Elba.

47. For art exhibitions at the Sanitary Fairs, see Elizabeth Milroy, "Avenue of Dreams: Patriotism and the Spectator at Philadelphia's Great Central Sanitary Fair," in *Making and Remaking Pennsylvania's Civil War*, ed. William Pencak and William Blair (University Park: The Pennsylvania State University Press, 2001), 23–57.

48. For Cushman, see *Dictionary of American Biography*, ed. Allen Johnson and Dumas Malone (New York: Charles Scribner's Sons, 1946), 5–6:1–2. For Sanitary Fair presentation albums, see *The Charlotte Cushman Collection*, exh. brochure (New York: Kennedy Galleries, 1976); and David Cassedy, *A Civil War Album*, exh. cat. (Philadelphia: The Schwarz Gallery, 1999).

49. For Hale, see Smith 1885, 484; and *Dictionary of American Biography*, ed. Allen Johnson and Dumas Malone (New York: Charles Scribner's Sons, 1946), 7–8:110. The late Mr. and Mrs. Thomas A. Brown acquired the Hale homestead in Elizabethtown and its contents that included the painting and the engraving (correspondence with the author).

50. Tuckerman 1867, 524.

51. Ferber, *Richards* (1986), 11, 74.

52. The ideological connotation of the panoramic format is discussed in Albert Boime, *The Magisterial Gaze: Manifest Destiny and American Landscape Painting, c. 1830–1865* (Washington, D.C.: Smithsonian Institution Press, 1991); Miller, *Empire* (1993); and McGrath, *Lake Placid* (1993).

53. "Philadelphia Art Notes," *The Round Table*, May 14, 1864, 344.

54. Tuckerman 1867, 524.

55. "Philadelphia Art Notes," *The Round Table*, September 30, 1865, 60.

56. Lawrie diary, Elizabethtown, August 27, 1865, collection of David Trout.

57. Durand, "Letter V" (1855), 146.

58. "New Picture by Richards," *Boston Daily Evening Transcript*, September 20, 1866, sec. 2, 4.

59. Lawrie diary, Saturday, July 4, 1868, quoted in *Lawrie* (1993), 14.

60. "The Whitney Collection," *New York Evening Post*, December 9, 1885. For Richards and Whitney's relationship and the impact of the sale, see Linda S. Ferber, *Tokens of a Friendship: Miniature Watercolors by William T. Richards*, exh. cat. (New York: The Metropolitan Museum of Art, 1982); and Ferber, *Richards* (2001).

61. Richards to George Whitney, Wyke Regis, Dorset, July 1, 1879, roll 2296, Richards Papers, AAA.

62. For an extended discussion of the topic, see Ferber, *Richards* (2001).

63. For information about the sketch panels, see Ferber, *Richards* (1980), 360–61, 384 n. 50, 387 n. 82.

64. For Anna Richards Brewster, see William Tenney Brewster's four volumes of her sketches published privately by the Marchbanks Press, Scarsdale, New York, between 1954 and 1960; Charles B. Ferguson, *He Knew the Sea, William Trost Richards, N.A. (1833–1905), and His Daughter Anna Richards Brewster (1870–1952)*, exh. cat. (New Britain, Conn.: The New Britain Museum of American Art, 1973); and Audrey Hall and Susan Brewster McClatchey, *Anna Richards Brewster*, exh. cat. (Philadelphia: Frank S. Schwarz & Son, 1990). Her papers are deposited at the Archives of American Art.

65. Placid Lake and the Shore Owners' Association of Lake Placid, *A Centennial History: 1893–1993* (Lake Placid, N.Y., 1993), 25.

IN SEARCH OF A NATIONAL LANDSCAPE

1. *Lake George*, 1855
Pencil on paper 7 x 11 7/8
Inscribed l.c.: [Lake] George
Signed and dated l.r. William T. Richards/24th June
Private collection

2. *[Panoramic view] Lake George,* 1855
Graphite on paper 3 7/8 x 12 1/16
Inscribed and dated l.l. Lake George/June 26, 1855
Private collection

3. *Lake George,* ca. 1855
Graphite and Chinese white on blue paper 1 7/8 x 5 7/8
Unsigned
Private collection

4. *Lake Champlain*, 1855
Graphite on paper 3 3/8 x 11 3/8
Dated and inscribed l.c. June 27, 1955/Lake Champlain
Private collection, courtesy of William Vareika Fine Arts, Newport, Rhode Island

5. *Pleasant Valley, Essex County*, 1855
Graphite on paper 4 15/16 x 11 7/8
Dated and inscribed l.r. Pleasant Valley/Essex County, N.Y./June 29th 1855
Private collection

6. *Plains of North Elba*, 1855
Graphite on paper 4 1/8 x 12 1/4
Dated and inscribed l.l. Plains of North Elba/Adirondack mts./July 2$^{nd}$ 1855
Private collection

7. *Indian Pass, Adirondacks*, 1855
Graphite on paper 10 7/8 x 8 1/4
Inscribed and dated l.c. Indian Pass—Adirondack/July 3$^{rd}$ 1855
The Adirondack Museum 2000.2.1

8. *Schroon River*, 1855
Graphite on paper 5 3/4 x 11 3/4
Inscribed and dated l.l. Schroon River/July 5th 1855
Private collection

9. *Pleasant Valley*, 1855
Graphite on paper 3 1/2 x 12
Inscribed l.l. Pleasant/Valley
Dated l.c. July 27th [or 29th]
Verso: part of another landscape
Private collection

10. *Essex Valley Adirondack Mountains*, 1855
Pencil on paper 4 7/8 x 11 7/8
Dated l.l. July 29th 1855
Private collection

11. *In the Adirondacks*, 1857
Oil on canvas 29 x 43 1/2
Signed and dated l.l. Wm T. Richards/1857
The Adirondack Museum 69.53.1 (211)

12. *A View in the Adirondacks*, ca. 1857
Oil on canvas 30 1/4 x 44 l/4
Signed and inscribed l.r. Wm. T. Richards/Phil.
Henry Art Gallery, Faye G. Allen Center for the Visual Arts

13. *Autumn in the Adirondacks*, 1857–58
Oil on canvas 24 1/8 x 36 1/2
Signed l.l. Wm. T. Richards
Private collection

14. *Lake George, opposite Caldwell*, 1857
Oil on canvas 19 x 27
Signed and dated l.r. Wm. T. Richards. 185[7]
Private collection

15. *Day Lilies by a Wooden Fence*, 1862
Graphite on paper 9 1/8 x 6
Dated l.l.c. June 26 1862
National Academy of Design, New York, Bequest of Mrs. William T. Richards

16. *The Adirondacks, Essex County*, ca. 1863
Pencil on paper 12 1/2 x 20 3/8
Unsigned
Brooklyn Museum of Art, Gift of Edith Ballinger Price 86.53.4

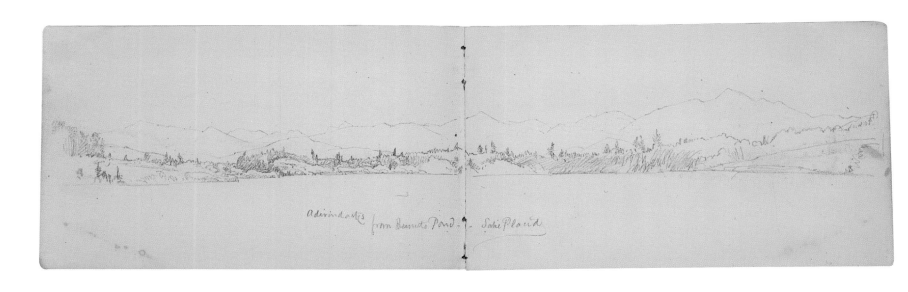

Adirondacks from Bennets Pond — Lake Placid

17a. *Adirondack Sketchbook*, June 14–19, 1863: E. Ausable River/June 19th 1863
Graphite on paper, no cover, unbound sections 4 3/4 x 8
Inscribed with various sites Keene, Bald Mountain, East Ausable River, Bennets Pond, Lake Placid,
Mt. McIntyre, Wilmington Notch, Whiteface Mountain, Jay
Brooklyn Museum of Art, Gift of Edith Ballinger Price 75.15.5

17b. *Adirondack Sketchbook*, June 14–19, 1863: Adirondacks from Bennets [sic] Pond, Lake Placid

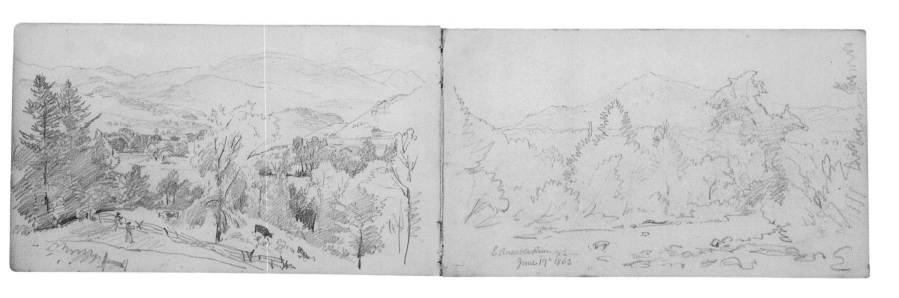

17c. *Adirondack Sketchbook*, June 14–19, 1863: June 20th, 1863

18. *Plant Study: Elizabethtown*, 1863
Graphite on paper 4 5/8 x 6 3/4
Dated and inscribed l.l. June 22/1863/Elizabethtown
Inscribed c.r. 3 ft high
Private collection

19. *Rock Cliffs*, 1863
Graphite on paper 9 5/8 x 6 1/8
Dated l.c. July 21st 1863
Iris & B. Gerald Cantor Center for Visual Arts at Stanford University 1992.55.36
Gift of M. J. and A. E. van Löben Sels

20. *Indian Pass, Adirondacks*, 1866
Charcoal and white chalk 19 x 23
Signed and dated l.l. W.T.R./1866
Arnot Art Museum 84.15, Purchased in part with funds from the Anderson-Evans Foundation, 1984

21. *Essex County in the Adirondacks*, 1862–66
Oil on paper 4 x 6
Unsigned
Private collection

22. *Elizabethtown*, 1862–66
Oil on paper 4 x 6 1/2
Unsigned
Private collection

23. *The Adirondack Mountains*, ca. 1864
Oil on paper 4 1/4 x 6 1/2
Unsigned
Inscribed verso: Adirondack Mts.
Private collection

24. *Adirondack Landscape*, 1864
Oil on canvas 22 x 31
Signed and dated l.r. Wm. T. Richards 1864
Private collection

25. *Bouquet Valley in the Adirondacks*, ca. 1864
Oil on canvas backed by panel 15 x 22
Signed l.r. Wm. T. Richards
Private collection

*26. John Brown's Grave (Sketch)*, ca. 1864
Oil on panel 9 x 14
Signed l.r. W. T. Richards
Private collection, courtesy of Caldwell Gallery, Manlius, New York

27. *A Valley in the Adirondacks*, ca. 1864
from the Charlotte Cushman Album
Oil on paper (mounted on Masonite) 6 1/4 x 9 3/4
Signed l.r. W. T. Richards.
Private collection

28. The Charlotte Cushman Album, 1864
Full green morocco quarto with ivory bosses
Bound by Pawson and Nicholson, Philadelphia
Collection of James B. Cummins Jr.

29. *Autumn in the Adirondacks*, 1865
Oil on canvas 25 x 36
Signed, dated, and inscribed l.r. Wm. T. Richards/Phila. 1865
Kenneth Lux Gallery

30. *The Bouquet Valley, Adirondacks*, 1866
Oil on canvas 25 x 42
Signed, dated, and inscribed l.l. Wm T. Richards/Phil. 1866
Biggs Museum of American Art

31. *Whiteface Mountain, Lake Placid*, n.d.
Oil on canvas board 9 3/4 x 15 3/8
Unsigned
National Academy of Design, New York, Bequest of Anna Richards Brewster, 1952

32. *Whiteface Mountain, Lake Placid*, 1904
Oil on board 9 1/2 x 15 1/2
Signed l.l. Wm T. Richards.
Private collection

33. *Lake Placid*, ca. 1904
Oil/gouache on board 9 7/8 x 15 5/8
Unsigned
Iris & B. Gerald Cantor Center for Visual Arts at Stanford University 1992.55.205
Gift of M. J. and A. E. van Löben Sels

34. *Lake Placid*, ca. 1904
Oil/gouache on board 9 7/8 x 15 5/8
Unsigned
Iris & B. Gerald Cantor Center for Visual Arts at Stanford University
1992.55.206
Gift of M.J. and A.E. van Löben Sels

35. *Lake Placid [looking south]*, ca. 1904
Watercolor on paper 5 1/4 x 8 3/8
Signed l.c. W. T. Richards
Private collection

36. *Curly Birch Camp, Lake Placid, New York*, ca. 1904
Anna Richards Brewster (1870–1952)
Oil on canvas 15 x 11
Unsigned
Private collection

"A WILD YET PLEASING LANDSCAPE":
*The Artists' Adirondacks, 1850–1870*

Cat. no. 55. *Village, Essex County, New York*, ca. 1867
Alexander Lawrie (1828–1917)
Oil on canvas 12 5/8 x 25
Signed and dated l.l. A. Lawrie/18[illegible]
95.22.1 (532), Purchase in memory of Patricia Carroll Fitzgerald Mandel

# "A WILD YET PLEASING LANDSCAPE":
## *The Artists' Adirondacks, 1850–1870*

CAROLINE M. WELSH

*A wild yet pleasing landscape, on which a painter's eye could not rest but with delight, and which, transferred to canvas, would make a picture of which any artist might be proud. . . .*[1]

IN THE MIDDLE YEARS of the nineteenth century the United States was confronted with a number of competing visions and vistas: burgeoning cityscapes; expanding mills and factory sites; and a seemingly endless expanse of natural grandeur embodied in mountains, forests, lakes, and rivers. All vied for attention as America's real image and each left an iconographic residue of town views, industrial and commercial architecture, and paintings to support its claim. These coexisting and competing realities of America burst on the international scene at London's Crystal Palace Exposition—the world's first great fair—in 1851. Here, under acres of steel and glass, was exhibited the work of all nations. It was America's debut before the world: McCormick's reaper, Newell's reputedly unpickable lock, Colt's revolver, and the stunning victory of the yacht *America* over England's best drew near universal praise and recognition. But not all the acclaim was for the innovative American products of industry and technology. Art, too, was recognized in the form of the sculpted body of Hiram Powers's (1805–1873) *Greek Slave.*

Back home, artists, long aware of America's uniqueness, invaded the realms of beauty so readily at hand in the mountains and forests of the Northeast from New York to Maine, where nature's wilderness romantically reinforced the nation's manifest mission and accomplishments. An unending procession of painters found in the splendor of nature a respite from the growing materialism of the nation's new urban and industrial landscapes and, in a variety of ways, helped leaven and soften those landscapes, making change more palatable for generations of Americans. Nature became the subject of much nineteenth-century art. America's wilderness regions fueled the artistic imagination and were laboratories for evolving ideas about the land and its role in American culture. Americans believed that wild nature embodied their country's deepest spiritual and democratic values. Few other places in the country served America's artists for so long or with so many subjects as the Adirondack wilderness in upstate New York. William Trost Richards's drawings and paintings of the region are the subject of this exhibition along with those of his contemporary artists who, like Richards, were inspired by the region to mirror it on canvas or paper.

The Adirondacks were the nation's third great wilderness, discovered by artists well after the Catskills to the north of New York City and the White Mountains of New Hampshire. In 1810 New York State was the second most populous in the Union with nearly one million inhabitants. To the north of Albany a large mountainous region lay virtually unknown and uninhabited. An account of 1784 described the place: "the country, lying to the West of these Lakes [George and Champlain] bounded on the North West by Canada River [the St. Lawrence], and on the South by the Mohawk River, called by the Indians Couxsachrage, which signifies the Dismal Wilderness or Habitation of Winter, is a triangular, high mountainous tract, very little known to the Europeans. . . ."[2] Until the third decade of the nineteenth century, the region was largely regarded to be so inhospitable that it was not worth exploring. Settlements had been made all around its periphery in the early 1800s, but few people had penetrated the heart of the wilderness, still called "Wild Unsettled Country" as late as 1823 on a map published by Carey and Lea.

Cat. no. 37. *Schroon Lake*, ca. 1846
Thomas Cole (1801–1848)
Oil on canvas 33 x 32
Signed l.c. TC
65.3.2 (101)

*savage grandeur, are pathless and inaccessible without a guide. The lakes, which are everywhere, and often strikingly beautiful, repel by the oppressive loneliness in which they slumber.*[3]

While this account more than likely exaggerated the actual experience, it very clearly created an impression for his readers about the nature of wilderness. On the other hand, the conventions of contemporary landscape painting arranged natural elements (trees, rocks, mountains, and water) found in the wilderness into pleasing compositions and thus constructed acceptable realities for their viewers. Nature was evaluated in terms of how much it "looked like a painting." Cole, describing the scenery he found near Schroon Lake in 1846, wrote: "I do not remember to have seen in Italy a composition of mountains so beautiful or pictorial as this glorious range of the Adirondack."[4] A distinct contrast to Noble's description of the environs of Long Lake, some fifty miles west of Schroon Lake.

Nineteenth-century artistic and literary descriptions of wild, uncultivated lands structured popular perceptions of wilderness and the Adirondacks as a place where it existed. Often the attitudes engendered were a mixture of hostility, fear, indifference, awe, and appreciation. Louis LeGrand Noble, Thomas Cole's biographer, chronicled a two-week trip Cole, two companions, and a guide made to "the Adirondack Mountains, and the wild shores of Long Lake" in September 1846. At the time, a trek of this magnitude was "one of the wildest and most fatiguing" east of the Mississippi. Noble described the country they encountered:

*The wilderness, haunted by the great moose, the wolf, the bear, the panther, seems almost interminable, and nearly houseless. The mountains, some of them reaching into the sky, ragged, rocky pinnacle, and robed with*

In the first decades of the nineteenth century, Cole and Asher B. Durand introduced an American style of landscape painting, popularly known after 1877 as the "Hudson River School."[5] The eighteenth-century notion of nature as background to human life was replaced by pictures that made the wild and solemn beauty of American wilderness the subject. And, according to Durand, landscape painting "will be great in proportion as it declares the glory of God, by representation of his works, and not of the works of man. . . ."[6] Cole's and Durand's pioneering forays in search of the picturesque along the Hudson River and in the Adirondacks by 1837 drew other artists to the northern wilderness. That same year the region was given its name by the New York State geologist Ebenezer Emmons when he conducted the geologic portion of the state's Natural History Survey.[7]

The English-born Cole made his first trip to the Adirondacks from his summer home in Catskill, New York, in 1826, visiting Lake George and the ruins of Fort Ticonderoga. Nine years later he went deeper into the mountains on a trip north of Lake George, which he recorded in his journal entry of October 7, 1835: "I have just returned from an excursion in search of the picturesque toward the head-waters of the Hudson. . . . The lake I found to be a beautiful sheet of water, overshadowed by sloping hills clothed with heavy forests."[8] The lake was Schroon Lake. Two years later, with his wife and artist-friend Durand, he was again at Schroon Lake, where he made several drawings of the scenery near Schroon Mountain (now known as Hoffman Mountain).

*Schroon Lake*, of about 1846 (cat. no. 37), is based on those drawings. It depicts a known site and its inhabitants but also conveys Cole's reactions to civilization's transformation of the wilderness. The log house and nearby sawmill, built in 1798 on the falls of the Paradox Lake outlet, was owned by Joseph Richards. He sold the lumber he milled in a shop attached to his home. The cemetery, in the clearing beyond the mill, is Severance Cemetery. Behind the house on the shore of the lake is a schoolhouse. The domesticated scene again belies the "savage grandeur" described by Noble. The imagery Cole employs underscores his belief in the harmonious relationship of man and nature. The blasted stump in the foreground signifies the taming of the wilderness, while the soaring mountains beneath a luminous sky reveal the presence of the divine. Here, according to Cole, we have "the sublimity of untamed wildness, and the majesty of the eternal mountains." On his last trip to the Adirondacks, in 1846, he pushed deeper into the interior all the way

Cat. no. 38. Untitled: Boulder and Trees, ca. 1858
Asher B. Durand (1796–1886)
Oil on canvas 25 x 20
Signed l.r. ABD
72.36.1 (281) Gift of Mrs. Douglas Delanoy

to Long Lake.

In June 1848 Durand returned to the Adirondacks with the artists John Frederick Kensett and John William Casilear (1811–1893). They traveled north beyond Lake George to Elizabethtown, ten miles west of Lake Champlain. Durand, in a letter to his son that June, wrote: "The mountain scenery is beautiful, superior to any I have met with in this country."[9] Durand visited Keene Valley, Lake Placid, and Lake George several times over his long career. His last visit was in 1877, at age eighty-one, to the Upper Ausable Lake in Keene Valley. His daughter described their visit:

*We hung the corner of his tent with rubber blankets and covered his bed of spruce and balsam boughs with a buffalo robe, and though it rained hard three nights there were no bad effects from it. Good campfires in front of the tent, being much in the pure air, and good meals kept him well. It was then he made studies for the picture now on the easel in his studio, and his last work.*[10]

Durand's objective naturalism, inspired by the advance of science and his training as an engraver, can be seen in the museum's untitled painting of a boulder and trees, of about 1858 (cat. no. 38). One of the first Americans to advocate painting out-of-doors in the presence of nature, Durand was also widely influential as a teacher. His "Letters on Landscape Painting," published in 1855 in the American art periodical *The Crayon*, admonished aspiring artists to draw the details of nature "with scrupulous fidelity."

The arresting beauty of Lake George was widely celebrated in eighteenth- and early-nineteenth-century diaries, journals, and travel accounts. "Everybody who has heard of American scenery has heard of Lake George. . . . the lake which, of all others, I most desired to see,"

Cat. no. 39. *Lake George*, 1856
John Frederick Kensett (1816–1872)
Oil on canvas 26 x 42
Signed l.r. JFK
65.79.1 (112)

Artists were attracted to Lake George because of this arresting physical beauty and the popular demand for images of it. Landscape painters created masterpieces in oil and watercolor. The printmakers William Henry Bartlett (1809–1854) and Harry Fenn (1845–1911) produced an enormous number of engravings while others produced lithographs after paintings. Still others documented the lake and its visitors for the popular press. Photographers produced images as works of art and for commercial purposes, all for a public eager to buy views of the picturesque lake. Indeed, by the 1850s the American public's appetite for pictures of American scenery was becoming inexhaustible.

Among amateur and professional artists, few found the lake as felicitous a subject as John Frederick Kensett. One of America's best-known and most successful landscape painters, he made at least a dozen formal compositions of the lake beginning in 1850. Kensett was strongly influenced by Cole and Durand, particularly by their beliefs in the religious and moral content of the landscape. His paintings expressed transcendental faith in "that beautiful harmony which God has created the universe." Kensett's *Lake George* of 1856 (cat. no. 39), with its classically balanced composition of mountains, shore, and serene lake, bathed in pink-gold light, conveys the sense of awe that natural perfection inspired in the artist. Kensett's paintings depict Nature at a particular time, place, and point of view, exactly observed and personally perceived. They celebrate a grand and majestically ordered Nature in paint. His light is delicate and serene; his mood pensive, quiet, and tranquil.

By midcentury, Lake George was no longer inaccessible wilderness; it was a scenic, although often crowded, vacation spot. Alfred Thompson Bricher's (1837–1908) views of Lake George result from two sketchbooks which survive from a visit in 1867. He depicted the lake in all its picturesque beauty as a vacationer's dream (cat. no. 40). His untitled view of about 1867 images the idyllic lake, ringed by woods and mountains beneath a sunny sky, and portrays a welcoming, peaceful, and congenial playground for post–Civil War tourists traumatized by the war. David Johnson's (1827–1908) paintings and drawings of the

wrote the English writer Harriet Martineau in 1835.[11] Seventeenth-century explorers on boats marveled at its virgin forests and pristine waters; eighteenth-century French, British, and American soldiers fought there; nineteenth-century travelers vacationed at the lake's elegant hotels as part of the American Grand Tour. Thomas Jefferson was so struck with the beauty of the scenery that he wrote his daughter Martha on May 31, 1791: "Lake George is, without comparison, the most beautiful water I ever saw. . . ."[12] The lake simultaneously epitomized nineteenth-century aesthetic concepts of the "sublime," the "beautiful," and the "picturesque." Its dramatic vistas and rugged mountains evoked awe and wonder and manifested nature as divine or sublime. Its pure and limpid waters expressed peace and harmony and exemplified the beautiful. Its aesthetic juxtaposition of mountains, water, islands, trees, and rocks provided the memorable view so eagerly sought by nineteenth-century travelers "touring in search of the picturesque."[13]

Cat. no. 40. Untitled: Boating Party on Lake George, ca. 1867
Alfred Thompson Bricher (1837–1908)
Oil on canvas 26 x 48
Signed l.r. A. T. Bricher
82.4.1 (443)

Cat. no. 41. *View from the Ruins of Fort George, Lake George*, 1873
David Johnson (1827–1908)
Oil on canvas 16 x 28
Signed and dated l.r. DJ '73
2001.23 (562) Gift in memory of Klari Horvath Erdoss and Bela K. Erdoss

1870s are rendered in the same manner. The grand hotels and abundant tourist attractions are not seen in his *View from the Ruins of Fort George, Lake George,* of 1873 (cat. no. 41), but steamboats and boating parties suggest the increased activity of the region. Uniform and luminous light, tightly controlled technique and composition, rich tonal colors in combination with extraordinarily realistic topographical, geological, and botanical details make Johnson's paintings of Lake George among his finest and relate his work to that of Richards.

DeWitt Clinton Boutelle (1820–1884), a self-taught landscapist from Troy, New York, was also strongly influenced by Cole and Durand. Boutelle's oil painting *The Sacandaga River at Hadley, New York*, 1867 (cat. no. 42), depicts a site to the south of Lake George that was painted almost fifty years earlier by the English artist William Guy Wall (1792–1864) and engraved by John Hill (1770–1850) for the *Hudson River Portfolio* (1821–22).

It was not until the middle of the nineteenth century that artists arrived in any numbers in the interior Adirondacks. By 1850 most prominent painters had been to the Catskills and White Mountains and had exhibited paintings of these subjects at the National Academy of Design in New York City. These two mountain areas were readily acces-

Cat. no. 42. *The Sacandaga River at Hadley, New York*, 1867
DeWitt Clinton Boutelle (1820–1884)
Oil on canvas 20 x 30
Signed l.l. Boutelle
90.2.1 (509)

Cat. no. 43. *A Hunting Party in the Woods,/In the Adirondack* [sic] *N.Y. State*, 1856
Frederick Rondel (1826–1892)
Oil on canvas 22 x 30
Signed l.r. F. Rondel
65.15.1 (104) Gift of The Shelburne Museum, Shelburne, Vt.,
through the generosity of J. Watson Webb

area communicated through paintings and prints attracted more artists and tourists. Artists, inspired by the dramatic Adirondack vistas, the limpid and pure light, and the rugged grandeur of the mountains, produced a substantial body of paintings, drawings, and watercolors as the century progressed. Many of these were reproduced as engravings or chromolithographs by publishers who recognized that the magnetism of the region for artists was also shared by the populace at large, particularly city dwellers who yearned to escape the growing complexities of urban life and an increasingly industrialized landscape. The new wealth in the cities also created a new class of art patron.

Known and unknown artists documented Adirondack scenery in the 1850s and 1860s. The Parisian artist Frederick Rondel (1826–1892) came to the United States in the 1840s. He settled first in Boston, and it is possible that he was introduced to the Adirondacks by the work of William James Stillman, co-editor of *The Crayon* and a landscape painter, whose painting *Study on Upper Saranac Lake, Adirondack Mountains* is dated 1854 (Ferber, fig. 6). Stillman returned to the Adirondacks in 1858 with members of Boston's renowned Saturday Club to camp at Follensby Pond near Tupper Lake. The ten participants and their activities of July 1858 were immortalized in Stillman's 1858 painting *Philosopher's Camp* and Ralph Waldo Emerson's poem *The Adirondacs: A Journal Dedicated to My Fellow Travellers in August, 1858.*[17] Rondel's *A Hunting Party in the Woods./In the Adirondac* [sic] *N.Y. State*, 1856 (cat. no. 43), depicts Rondel himself with a convivial group of gentlemen-sportsmen in a forest clearing in the Adirondack wilderness. The format and subject matter of Rondel's picture are similar to Stillman's. The fact that it predates it may further substantiate the possibility that Stillman and Rondel knew each other's work. The tranquil forest primeval provides both pictures with the harmonious setting for reaping nature's psychic and actual rewards.

James Cameron (1817–1882), a Scottish portrait and landscape painter, immigrated and first settled in Philadelphia. Nothing is known about his Adirondack experience except the existence of a painting called *Long Lake*, of about 1855 (cat. no. 44). This work was owned by Farrand N. Benedict, a professor of mathematics at the University of Vermont in the 1840s and owner of a large tract of land near Long Lake in the central Adirondacks. According to a Burlington, Vermont,

sible to the artistic centers of New York, Albany, and Boston, whereas the Adirondacks' rugged terrain and remoteness made the region more difficult to reach.[14] In 1861 the New York periodical *The Friend's Intelligencer* carried an article describing a trip taken in the summer of 1859, which stated: "The Adirondack region is often spoken of in social circles with a vague sense of its gloom, its privacy and its grandeur, just as we speak of the . . . Ural mountains, which we read of in books, but never expect to visit."[15] *Appleton's Journal of Popular Literature, Science and Art* on September 24, 1870, still perpetuated the notion that the Adirondacks of the 1850s were "almost as unknown as the interior of Africa. There were few huts or houses there, and a very few visitors."[16] After 1850 improved transportation and increased knowledge of the

Cat. no. 44. *Long Lake*, ca. 1855
James Cameron (1817–1882)
Oil on canvas 22 x 42
Signed l.c. J. Cameron
69.91.1 (213) Gift of Farrand Northrup Benedict Jr.

advertisement, on January 23, 1855, the artist from Philadelphia was there at this date: "Three beautiful paintings, (two landscapes—Avalanche Lake and Long Lake, N.Y. and a portrait) by James Cameron, of Philadelphia, are now at the store of Brinsmaid and Hildreth, and will remain there for a short time previous to being sent South. The public are invited to come and see them."[18]Any connection to Richards is unknown.

Works of art on paper are ephemeral survivals of artists' ventures in the wilderness. Jervis McEntee's drawing *Wood's Cabin on Rackett* [sic] *Lake*, 1851 (fig. 17), pictures the cabin of Josiah Wood, one of Raquette Lake's first settlers at a time when few other people had found this spot. McEntee, aged twenty-three, recorded his impressions of his adventure in his diary, sketchbook, and for the newspaper *Rondout Courier* on July 18, 1851. In his diary, he described the cabin on July 6 as "comfortable" and "built of logs with a bark covered porch in front. It stands on a gentle elevation about fifty yards from the lake [and wood] has a very good garden. . . ."[19] Joel T. Headley, in his 1849

account *The Adirondacks*, described the same huts as "looking like oases in the desert, occupied by two men, who dwell thus shut out from the civilized life."[20] This drawing predates Richards's July 3, 1855, drawing of Indian Pass (cat. no. 7), an equally lonely but more rugged site.

In 1850 American landscape painting was a powerful medium for conveying national, cultural, and religious ideas. During the first half of the nineteenth century, transcendentalist thinkers led by Emerson and Hudson River School artists inspired by Cole and Durand vested the American landscape with spiritual and regenerative powers through verbal and painted images of idealized wilderness scenery. Americans began to appreciate the natural beauty of their land even as the pioneering spirit—which saw the wilderness as an obstacle to be tamed—

Fig. 17. *Wood's Cabin on Rackett* [sic] *Lake*, 1851
Jervis McEntee (1828–1892). Pencil 11 x 13
76.77.1 Gift of Mrs. Jacqueline Schonbrun and sons in memory of Stanley I. Schonbrun

Cat. no. 45. *A Twilight in the Adirondacks*, 1864
Sanford Robinson Gifford (1823–1880)
Oil on canvas 24 x 36
Signed l.r. S. R. Gifford
63.124.2 (90)

mon eye."[21] There are four known versions of Gifford's composition depicting a shoreline silhouetted between a radiant twilight sky and its reflection in a lake with a camping scene on the shore. The campers are likely to be the artist, his colleagues McEntee and Richard William Hubbard (1816–1888), and their guide. The Adirondack Museum's painting is the largest version. It was exhibited at the National Academy of Design in 1864 and at the Philadelphia Centennial Exhibition in 1876. At its first exhibition, the *New York Evening Post* exclaimed that "Gifford has never painted a picture of more exquisite gradations than this."[22]

Deep in the heart of the Adirondack high peaks, a rural hamlet set in a tranquil river-valley in the midst of exceptionally dramatic mountainous terrain became a locus for artistic activity. Keene Flats was one of the first places in the region to be inhabited. Settled in 1797, it opened its first hotel in 1823. Artists discovered the valley about 1850. J. A. Martin (n.d.), an artist known only by this painting, titled on the canvas and

pushed westward to conquer the continent. Landscape artists influenced the way post–Civil War Americans viewed their land and prompted scores of tourists to head for the country in search of nature's picturesque sites and vistas.

This idealized landscape convention remained popular because of a persistent belief in the spiritual power of nature and the role of the artist to depict it. Sanford Robinson Gifford's *A Twilight in the Adirondacks*, 1864, is a masterful example (cat. no. 45). In 1881 John F. Weir (1841–1926), director of the Yale School of Fine Arts, wrote that "Gifford loved the light. His finest impressions were those derived from the landscape, where the air is charged with an effulgence of irruptive and glowing light. . . . He was unerringly profound in his insight into that which was most truly nature, into those potent truths that underlie the superficial aspects which engage the common mind or attract the com-

stretcher *A View of the Valley of Keene, Essex County, 1851* (cat. no. 46), documents, in the manner of Cole, Keene Valley at about this time.

Artists came to Keene Valley as part of summer sketching trips to the Hudson River Valley, the Catskills, and Lake George. After the Civil War, they came for longer stays and built studios. By the 1880s, the area was so popular with painters and their students

Cat. no. 46. *A View of the Valley of Keene, Essex County*, 1851
J. A. Martin (n.d.)
Oil on canvas 16 x 20
Signed and dated l.r. J. A. Martin 1851 98.50.1 (54

that the popular magazines of the day called Keene Valley an "Artist's Mecca" and a "Haunt for Landscape Painters." Orson Phelps, a local guide and entrepreneur, claimed "Keene Flats . . . was discovered by the artist. With pencil he made pictures and sent them back to the cities, to be noticed in the drawing rooms and public halls. Visitors began to arrive. Each one brought three next year. . . . [The artists] are quiet people, who see more beauty in a summer cloud hanging for a moment on the mountain summit than others. . . ."[23]

The abundance of landscape vistas in and around Keene Valley was irresistible. Artists captured forest interiors, the Ausable River roaring through a gorge or meandering tranquilly through the valley, the Upper and Lower Ausable Lakes lying between lofty peaks. Landscape painters celebrated the valley's beauty in all its moods and seasons and, in the process, helped to stimulate a boom in tourism and wilderness appreciation.

Roswell Morse Shurtleff (1838–1915) was most responsible for popularizing Keene Valley as an "Artist's Mecca." Born in New Hampshire, Shurtleff visited the Adirondacks as early as 1858. He came again in 1860 when he met Arthur Fitzwilliam Tait (1819–1905), the renowned painter of American sporting scenes, at Bay Pond in the northwestern Adirondacks, and again in 1867 after he saw paintings of the region by his Hartford colleague and friend, John Lee Fitch (1836–1895). From the summer of 1868 until his death in 1915, Keene Valley was his home and studio for much of each year. By 1910 he counted forty umbrellas near his studio, "with artists, canvas and paints beneath each one."[24] Shurtleff was known nationally for his glowing forest scenes.

In 1859 Keene Flats was described thus: "Encircled by rugged mountains, these flats, in their emerald beauty are most refreshing to the eye; the land is here rich and easily tilled, and neat farm houses painted white, with green blinds and red roofs, form very agreeable contrasts with the dilapidated and unpainted edifices which we have encountered

Cat. no. 47. *Keene Valley, Adirondacks*, 1861
Joseph Vollmering (1810–1887)
Oil on canvas 16 x 22
Unsigned
97.48.1 (540) Gift of Richard T. Button

for several miles back."[25] These words could describe the German-born Joseph Vollmering's (1810–1887) *Keene Valley, Adirondacks*, of 1861 (cat. no. 47). Vollmering knew Durand, Casilear, and Kensett. It is possible that they introduced him to the valley and that he accompanied one or more of them there.

Another early view of Keene Valley is William Hart's (1823–1894) untitled night scene dated 1861 (cat. no. 48). Night scenes are rare in midcentury American landscape painting. This small oil shows the valley landscape bathed in the silvery light of the full moon, which underlies the eerie loneliness of the solitary house in the mountainous wilderness. His younger brother James M. Hart (1828–1901) painted a number of Adirondack scenes in addition to collaborating with Tait as the

Cat. no. 48. Untitled: Night Scene, 1861
William Hart (1823–1894)
Oil on canvas 8 x 16
Signed l.r. Wm. Hart
70.198.1 (233)

Cat. no. 49. Untitled: View on Loon Lake, 1862
James M. Hart (1828–1901)
Oil on canvas 19 x 32
Signed l.r. J. M. Hart
67.220.6 (184)

landscape painter for Tait's animal expertise. The museum's untitled picture of Loon Lake from 1862 (cat. no. 49) demonstrates Hart's abilities as a sensitive depicter of nature's details as well as animal poses.

The Hart brothers were from Albany and spent many summers in the valley for their art. Another Albanian and student of James was Homer Dodge Martin. He was sent to the region first by his teacher in 1864. His many Adirondack pictures include several in the museum's collection. *Mountain View on the Saranac*, 1868 (cat. no. 50), was commissioned by the periodical *Every Saturday*. The wood engraving after this painting illustrates an article entitled "Adventures in the Wilderness," written by William H.H. Murray in 1869 to lure tourists to the Adirondacks. Whereas the print catalogued the topography, the painting is fraught with drama, the rugged scenery on the Saranac River shrouded with forbidding atmosphere.

George Henry Smillie (1840–1921) was the fifth child of the noted American engraver James Smillie (1807–1885). Like his older brother James David (1833–1909) and his father, he was an engraver, etcher, and painter. From the early 1860s until the 1880s, the two brothers' careers and lives were closely intertwined as they traveled to the same picturesque locations for subject matter and occupied adjacent studios in New York City. They made the first of three consecutive trips to the Adirondacks in the summer of 1868. Staying at Beede's popular boardinghouse (now the site of the Ausable Club) in Keene Valley, the brothers toured and sketched mountain and valley sites. The Smillie brothers' strong compositional sense and their ability to produce precise topographical detail along with their dramatic use of color, link them stylistically to Richards (cat. nos. 51, 52).

A student of Durand, Samuel Colman (1832–1920) was a prominent nineteenth-century landscape and genre painter as well as a designer of wallpaper and fabrics. He worked in both oil and watercolor and was the first president of the American Society of Painters in Watercolor, founded in 1866. He, too, visited Keene Valley with fellow watercolorist James David Smillie in 1868 and may have executed his romantic view of fishing on the Ausable River at this time (cat. no. 53). In this painting, Colman reiterates the aesthetic vocabulary of the sublime as an awesome natural setting overwhelms a fisherman. The contrast

Cat. no. 50. *Mountain View on the Saranac*, 1868
Homer Dodge Martin (1836–1897)
Oil on canvas 30 x 56
Signed l.r. H. D. Martin
71.46.1 (262)

Cat. no. 51. *Ausable Lake, Adirondack Mountains*, 1868
George Henry Smillie (1840–1921)
Oil on canvas 11 x 18
Signed l.r. Geo. H. Smillie
74.29.2 (377)

Cat. no. 52. *Top of Giant's Leap, Adirondacks*, 1869
James David Smillie (1833–1909)
Watercolor on paper 20 x 13
Unsigned
62.9.1 (60) Gift of Mrs. Harold K. Hochschild

between the massive geologic scale of the rocks and the minute scale of the man is made more dramatic by the light and atmosphere veiling the ravine. This is not a picture about fishing but rather one about wilderness and nature and man's place in it.

Horace Wolcott Robbins Jr. (1842–1904) believed, like Richards and Durand, in the adherence to "close study of facts and details . . . careful drawing and local coloring" to enable the artist to be "the interpreter of Nature."[26] This luminous, quiet scene of cleared fields, grazing sheep, and winding road below the jagged silhouette of the Wolf Jaw Mountains pictures a civilized Eden in contrast to the horrors of Civil War battlefields Robbins had recently witnessed (cat. no. 54). Robbins went to Keene Valley in 1863 at the suggestion of his teacher, James M. Hart. In the late 1870s he purchased property on the west side of the valley, where he continued to capture its mountain and river scenery in both oil and watercolor.

Arthur Parton (1842–1914) moved from his birthplace of Hudson, New York, in 1859 to Philadelphia, where he studied landscape paint-

Cat. no. 53. Untitled: Ausable River, ca. 1869
Samuel Colman (1832–1920)
Oil on canvas 30 x 40
Signed l.r. Sam. l Colman
72.160.3 (311) Gift of Harold K. Hochschild

Cat. no. 54. Untitled: Wolf Jaw Mountain, 1863
Horace Wolcott Robbins Jr. (1842–1904)
Oil on canvas 13 x 22
Signed l.l. Robbins
74.292.1 (376)

ing with William Trost Richards for several years. In 1864 he settled in and worked out of various studios in Manhattan. He first visited the Adirondacks in 1866 and then made regular summer visits to Keene Valley and the Ausable Lakes until he bought a cottage in the Catskills about 1880. Parton was an experienced angler and was so described in a reminiscence, "the best fishing fellow you could wish to meet . . . and how he can paint!"[27] One can imagine that he often saw this scene of mist rising off a lake from the perspective of a fishing boat (fig. 18).

Elizabethtown, a village twelve miles east of Keene Valley, also attracted artists for summer

Fig. 18. *In the Adirondacks*, ca. 1866
Arthur Parton (1842–1914)
Oil on canvas 21 x 29. 68.169.1 (202)
Gift of Harold K. Hochschild

sojourns. From there they could travel to the valley, climb in the High Peaks, or head off to Lake Placid to the north and west with relative ease. *History of Essex County* (1885) describes the local beauty and picturesque siting of the village:

*There are few spots to be found anywhere more pleasantly adapted by nature for the site of a rural village. The road by which the lovely valley is reached from Westport winds between lofty rugged peaks, which increase in natural wildness and grandeur as one travels westward, until on surmounting an eminence the valley lies spread before us in all its romantic beauty. It is almost surrounded by some of the grandest*

83

Cat. no. 55. *Village, Essex County, New York*, ca. 1867
Alexander Lawrie (1828–1917)
Oil on canvas 12 5/8 x 25
Signed and dated l.l. A. Lawrie/18[illegible]
95.22.1 (532) Purchase in memory of Patricia Carroll Fitzgerald Mandel

Cat. no. 56. *The Adirondack Mountains, near Elizabethtown,*
*Essex Co., N.Y. in 1866*
John Henry Dolph (1835–1903)
Oil on canvas 27 x 48
Signed l.l. J. H. Dolph 66.24.1 (117)

*peaks in the Adirondacks. . . . No wonder the pioneers who first looked down on this beautiful spot named it Pleasant Valley. . . .*[28]
It was here that Richards based himself in 1855 and between 1862 and 1868.

Alexander Lawrie first came to the Adirondacks in 1863 with his friend and studiomate Richards after Lawrie had been wounded in the Civil War. Born in New York City, he studied art at the National Academy of Design, in Philadelphia from 1850 to 1854, then in Europe at Düsseldorf, Paris, and Florence, returning to Philadelphia in 1858. In the Adirondacks, Lawrie hiked as well as painted the High Peaks and was among the first to climb Giant Mountain. His paintings of views seen from the top of Giant are dated 1867, one year after the first trail was cut. His diary entries between 1863 and 1869 recorded Adirondack sojourns away from Elizabethtown to paint many views of the Bouquet Valley, Lake Champlain, the Saranac Lakes, Lake Placid, and Keene Valley.[29] On Saturday, July 19, 1863, his diary states: "I leave this beautiful Bolton [near Lake George] tomorrow for Elizabethtown, Essex County, N.Y., where my good friend W. T. [William Trost] Richards, the landscape painter, is." He goes on to note: "Have made several interesting acquaintances while here. Mr. Ed Stossen and Mr.

A. [Asher] B. Durand and family. . . . Mr. Durand is staying here for the summer making studies. . . ." The "September 22, [1863] Elizabethtown" entry states that the artists Gifford, McEntee, and Hubbard passed through. He continues: "For the nine weeks here I have worked closely nine hours nearly every day. Out of doors nearly every day with little or no company except W.T. Richards, who has been quite kind to me; . . ." He also mentions the presence of Hermann Fuechsel (1833–1915). Several entries in 1868 describe various sketching expeditions or walks with the artists Richards, George B. Wood Jr. (1832–1909), also of Philadelphia, Durand, and Fuechsel.[30] *Village, Essex County, New York*, of about 1867 (cat. no. 55), is likely a depiction of the Bouquet River outside Elizabethtown, perhaps from Wood Hill, one of Lawrie's favorite spots.

John Henry Dolph (1835–1903) painted *The Adirondack Mountains, near Elizabethtown, Essex Co., N.Y. in 1866* (cat. no. 56), a view similar to Lawrie's 1867 grisaille *View from Wood Mountain of Valley of Boquet River* (The Hand House, Elizabethtown, N.Y.). Born in Fort Ann, near Lake George, Dolph began his artistic career as a portrait painter in Michigan. In the 1860s he made the Adirondack and New Hampshire landscape his subject.

Lake Placid, northwest of Pleasant Valley and Keene Valley, was another popular destination for artists. Whiteface Mountain dominated the lakescape, as can be seen in Augustus Rockwell's (1822–1882) *Whiteface Mountain from Lake Placid, Essex Co.* executed in 1873 (cat. no. 57). Rockwell also painted around Old Forge, the southwest entry to the Adirondacks, as did Thomas Worthington Whittredge (1820–1910). His *View of the Fourth Lake, Old Forge*, of about 1861 (fig. 19), details not only what he saw in nature but what he felt about the solitary quietude of Fourth Lake. He, too, was moved by Durand's art and teachings to paint the American landscape.

Another mecca for artists was near Minerva, south and west of Keene Valley. Here the terrain was much less spectacular, but the opportunities for hunting and fishing were rich. By 1859 sportsmen and artists frequently boarded at a farm owned by

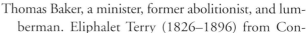

Cat. no. 57. *Whiteface Mountain from Lake Placid, Essex Co.*, 1873
Augustus Rockwell (1822–1882)
Oil on canvas 17 x 14
Signed on verso: Rockwell, Pt.
68.125.1 (197)

Thomas Baker, a minister, former abolitionist, and lumberman. Eliphalet Terry (1826–1896) from Connecticut was among them. An avid sportsman, he often vacationed and painted in the Adirondacks, White Mountains, Maine, and Canada with fellow Hartford artists Winslow Homer and Fitch. Terry painted Baker's log homestead, detailing its primitive structures in a newly cleared site thus underlining the frontier quality of the Adirondacks in *Baker's Farm*, 1859 (cat. no. 58). We surmise from the number of pictures that survive that the farm's beautiful setting in a ring of mountains caught his artistic fancy as well as that of nineteenth-century art buyers, travelers, and sportsmen. Terry returned to Baker's regularly after the family stopped running the boardinghouse. In 1886 he built his own cottage as one of the original and founding members of a private club called

Fig. 19. *View of the Fourth Lake, Old Forge*, ca. 1861. Thomas Worthington Whittredge (1820–1910). Oil on canvas 11 x 17. 66.87.1 (133)

Cat. no. 58. *Baker's Farm*, 1859
Eliphalet Terry (1826–1896)
Oil on canvas 19 x 30
Unsigned
L13.1998.1 Courtesy North Woods Club

Cat. no. 59. *Still Hunting on the First Snow: A Second Shot*, 1855
Arthur Fitzwilliam Tait (1819–1905)
Oil on canvas 54 x 76
Signed l.r. A. F. Tait
65.36.10 (110) Gift of Mr. and Mrs. Walter Hochschild

the North Woods Club, situated at Baker's Farm clearing. After Terry's death in 1896, Homer took over the cabin and used it until the year before his death in 1910.[31]

In contrast to the "beautiful view," a more prosaic subject attracted artists and tourists to the Adirondacks, namely, camping in the woods. Evocative of the region, camping scenes depict urban sportsmen relaxing in a forest glen with their guides near a lean-to or some other shelter. Men usually are seen congenially eating, drinking, or smoking rather than hunting or fishing. An Adirondack guideboat, a native canoe, a pack basket, a fishing rod and gun, and other accouterments of sport become tools of the guide and sportsman alike. The Adirondacks, from earliest times, were promoted as a remote and trackless wilderness inhabited by rustic innkeepers, guides, and frontiersmen subsisting in a forested kingdom amid an abundance of fish, waterfowl,

and woodland creatures. New Yorkers of the Gilded Age viewed the Adirondacks as a vast, aristocratic game preserve. To the gentleman-sportsman, no other region of the eastern United States compared with the North Country for hunting and fishing in the second half of the nineteenth century. Works of art did much to reinforce and perpetuate that impression.

Arthur Fitzwilliam Tait was the quintessential image-maker for the allure of the sporting aspect of the region. Tait immigrated to America from England in 1850 and established himself as a painter, having already achieved success as a lithographer. His discovery of the Adirondacks in 1852 determined his subject matter for the next thirty years. An ardent sportsman and lover of the outdoors, Tait lived in the region for extended periods of time near Chateaugay, Raquette, and Long lakes. His images of animals and sporting adventures were among the best known in nineteenth-century America thanks to Currier and Ives, whose lithographs of Tait's paintings helped popularize the Adirondacks as a sportsman's paradise.[32]

*Still Hunting on the First Snow: A Second Shot*, of 1855 (cat. no. 59), one of the largest paintings ever created by the artist, exemplifies Tait's artistic prowess and his love of hunting. Tait's original title for the work at the 1855 exhibition at the National Academy of Design was *A Second Shot: Still Hunting on the First Snow in the Chateaugay Forest*. He portrays himself in buckskins center stage about to pull the trigger. Tait learned Adirondack woodcraft and how to camp and hunt—including the technique of still hunting—from descendants of the first settlers of the Chateaugay lakes region.[33] The variety of game there provided him with much subject matter as he perfected his considerable talents in rendering fur, fin, and horn. Louis Maurer and Fanny Palmer reproduced a near-copy of the scene on a lithographic stone. The print was published by Nathaniel Currier as *Deer Shooting "On the Shattagee,"* in 1856.

Tait painted his own shanty on Constable Point (now Antlers Point) on Raquette Lake in *A Good Time Coming*, 1862 (cat. no. 60). He moved to Raquette Lake in the summer of 1860 because the Chateaugay environs had become too developed by entrepreneurs who, backed by wealthy patrons, built resort hotels. Raquette Lake remained picturesque, remote, and unsettled. With his guides Calvin Parker, Jim

Blossom, and Josiah Blossom, Tait camped there for nearly a decade. Tait recorded the identity of one of the figures in this painting in his Register of Paintings. The gentleman holding the bottle was John C. Force, a Brooklyn restaurateur and collector of Tait's paintings. Two of the other figures were guides, one bringing freshly caught fish to the campsite and the other cooking over the fire. Among the gear brought for comfortable camping, hunting, and fishing was a wooden packing case of wine bottles. The label reveals that they were from Tait's good friend John Osborn, a Brooklyn liquor importer. These acknowledgments of patron and friend provide interesting insights into the relationship of nineteenth-century artists and their patrons. Currier and Ives published this image as a hand-colored lithograph in 1863.[34]

America's devotion to natural beauty accelerated as the nineteenth century progressed, particularly as the landscape became increasingly defaced. Artists' images of a landscape exploited and compromised by logging and mining provided powerful aesthetic arguments for the conservation of the land. As early as 1835 Thomas Cole had decried the destruction of the landscape. In his "Complaint of the Forest" he notes: "We feed ten-thousand fires! In one short day/The woodland growth of centuries is consumed. . . ."[35] His concern was enjoined by the wilderness advocates George Perkins Marsh, Verplanck Colvin, S. H. Hammond, and the artist Julian Rix (1850–1903). Businessmen echoed the complaint when diminution of Adirondack and Catskill watersheds threatened downstate water power and canal interests. In the Adirondacks, these concerns came to fruition with the establishment of the Forest Preserve (1885) and the Adirondack Park (1892) as public places of wilderness.

William Trost Richards and his fellow artists in the 1850s and 1860s have pictured on canvas and paper Hammond's eloquent words of 1860:

*Their bare and rocky summits glistening in the sunlight, while near still the hills rise. . . . Here and there a valley winds away among the highlands, along which mountain streams come bounding down. . . . The rugged and sublime, with the placid and beautiful, in natural scenery, are*

Cat. no. 60. *A Good Time Coming*, 1862
Arthur Fitzwilliam Tait (1819–1905)
Oil on canvas 20 x 30
Signed l.c. A. F. Tait
63.37.1 (76) Gift of Harold K. Hochschild

*magnificently mingled in these surroundings. . . .*[36]

These artists came to the Adirondacks to hunt and fish, explore wild nature, and to hone their skills at transcribing and interpreting the Adirondack wilderness. In all of these paintings people and their activities, where present in the scene, are dwarfed by their natural surroundings. Tait is the exception; in his art sportsmen either hunting or fishing share equal billing with the flora and fauna in their sylvan settings. But in all cases, nature is the underlying if not primary subject. The natural grandeur of the American land, particularly the Adirondacks, was taking center stage in American art. William Trost Richards extended this effort as he instilled in his Adirondack pictures new visual meanings in his search for a "national landscape."

1. S. H. Hammond, *Wild Northern Scenes; or, Sporting Adventures with the Rifle and the Rod* (New York: Derby & Jackson, 1860), 191.

2. Thomas Pownall, *Topographical Description of the Dominions of the United States of America*, ed. Lois Mulkearn (Pittsburgh: University of Pittsburgh Press, 1949), 50–51, as quoted in Philip Terrie, *Forever Wild: Environmental Aesthetics and the Adirondack Forest Preserve* (Philadelphia: Temple University Press, 1985), 108.

3. Louis LeGrand Noble, *The Life and Works of Thomas Cole*, ed. Elliot S. Vessel (1853; reprint, Cambridge, Mass.: Harvard University Press, 1964), 280.

4. Ibid., 77.

5. See Kevin J. Avery, "A Historiography of the Hudson River School," in John K. Howat et al., *American Paradise: The World of the Hudson River School*, exh. cat. (New York: The Metropolitan Museum of Art and Harry N. Abrams, 1987), 3–8.

6. Asher B. Durand, "Letters on Landscape Painting" (1855), as quoted in Barbara Novak, *Nature and Culture* (New York and Toronto: Oxford University Press, 1980), 9.

7. Ebenezer Emmons, *New York State Natural History Survey Report*, 1838, quoted in Frank Graham Jr., *The Adirondack Park: A Political History* (New York: Alfred A. Knopf, 1978), 12.

8. Quoted in Noble, *The Life and Works of Thomas Cole*, 151–52.

9. Quoted in Robin Pell, *Keene Valley: The Landscape and Its Artists*, exh. cat. (New York: Gerald Peters Gallery, 1994), unpaginated.

10. Margaret C. O'Brien, "Durand in the Adirondacks," *Adirondack Life* 2 (summer 1971):

39. The painting is *Sunset: Souvenir of the Adirondacks*, in the collection of the New-York Historical Society.

11. Harriet Martineau, *Retrospect of Western Travel* (London: Saunders and Otley, 1838), 2:221, as quoted in Russell P. Bellico, *Chronicles of Lake George Journeys in War and Peace* (Fleischmanns, N.Y.: Purple Mountain Press, 1995), 274.

12. Thomas Jefferson to Martha Jefferson Randolph, May 31, 1791, in *The Writings of Thomas Jefferson*, ed. Paul Leicester Ford (New York: G. P. Putnam, 1904), 6:264.

13. Sue Rainey, *Creating "Picturesque America": Monument to the Natural and Cultural Landscape* (Nashville and London: Vanderbilt University Press, 1994), 22–31.

14. Patricia C.F. Mandel, *Fair Wilderness: American Paintings in the Collection of the Adirondack Museum* (Blue Mountain Lake, N.Y.: The Adirondack Museum, 1990), 27–28.

15. "An Excursion to the Adirondack Mountains," *The Friend's Intelligencer*, 1861, 650. The Adirondack Museum Library.

16. "Adirondack Scenery," *Appleton's Journal of Popular Literature, Science and Art* 4, no. 78 (September 24, 1870): 364–65.

17. This poem commemorates the 1858 Adirondack visit of a group of Concord-Cambridge scholars and luminaries, including the Harvard scientist Louis Agassiz, the poet and editor James Russell Lowell, and the artist and journalist William James Stillman. Emerson's poem was published in *May-Day and Other Poems* (Boston: Ticknor and Fields, 1867), 41–62. See Alfred Donaldson's two-volume *History of the Adirondacks* (Harrison, N.Y.: Harbor Hill Books, 1977), for a description of Philosopher's Camp in 1858.

18. *Burlington (Vt.) Daily Free Press*, January 23, 1855. The Adirondack Museum Artist's Files.

19. Jervis McEntee diary and sketchbook, reel D9, frame 589, Archives of American Art, Smithsonian Institution, Washington, D.C.

20. Joel T. Headley, *The Adirondack; or, Life in the Woods*, a facsimile of the 1849 edition, with later added chapters and a new introduction by Philip G. Terrie (Harrison, N.Y.: Harbor Hill Books, 1982), 203–4.

21. Address given by the artist John Ferguson Weir, as quoted in *American Paradise*, 220.

22. Ila Weis, *Poetic Landscape: The Art and Experience of Sanford R. Gifford* (Newark: University of Delaware Press; London and Toronto: Associated University Presses, 1987), 241–42.

23. Quoted in Pell, *Keene Valley: The Landscape and Its Artists*.

24. Quoted in Mandel, *Fair Wilderness*, 104, from *American Art News* 9, no. 3 (October 29, 1910): 4.

25. "An Excursion to the Adirondack Mountains," 1861, 667. The Adirondack Museum Library.

26. George W. Sheldon, *American Painters* (New York: D. Appleton and Co., 1879), 134.

27. Quoted in Mandel, *Fair Wilderness*, 94, from George Gould to his father, Jay, from Catskill County in "Bye the Bye on Wall Street," in *Wall Street Evening Edition*, May 23, 1923, in National Academy of Design Archives, New York.

28. H. P. Smith, ed., *History of Essex County* (Syracuse, N.Y.: D. Mason & Co., 1885), 487.

29. Peggy O'Brien, "Alexander Lawrie (1828–1917) Adirondack Artist," *Adirondac*, May 1984, 24–29.

30. Mary Ann Goley and Robin Pell, *Alexander Lawrie, Views of Essex County, New York*, exh. cat. (Washington, D.C.: Federal Reserve Board Fine Arts Program, 1993), 7–22.

31. Juliette Baker Kellogg diary, MS 61-83, Adirondack Museum Library; and Leila Fosburgh Wilson, "The North Woods Club, 1886–1986: One Hundred Years in the Adirondack Wilderness," typescript, 1986, The Adirondack Museum Library.

32. Warder Cadbury with Henry F. Marsh, *Arthur Fitzwilliam Tait: Artist in the Adirondacks* (Newark: University of Delaware Press; London and Toronto: Associated University Presses, 1986), 40–41.

33. Local methods of hunting varied with the season: in summer dogs were employed to drive the deer out of the woods into lakes, where the hunter and his guide would kill the animal from a boat; in fall hunters, singly or in small groups, quietly stalked or remained still to shoot the animal. Ibid., 41.

34. Ibid., 67.

35. Thomas Cole, "Essay on American Scenery," 1835, as quoted in William H. Truettner and Allan Wallach, *Thomas Cole: Landscape into History*, exh. cat. (New Haven and London: Yale University Press; Washington, D.C.: National Museum of American Art, 1994), 67.

36. Hammond, *Wild Northern Scenes*, 40–41.

# CHECKLIST

1. *Lake George*, 1855
Pencil on paper 7 x 11 7/8
Inscribed l.c.: [Lake] George
Signed and dated l.r. William T. Richards/
24th June
Private collection

2. *[Panoramic view] Lake George*, 1855
Graphite on paper 3 7/8 x 12 1/16
Inscribed and dated l.l. Lake George/June 26,
1855
Private collection

3. *Lake George*, ca. 1855
Graphite and Chinese white on blue paper
1 7/8 x 5 7/8
Unsigned
Private collection

4. *Lake Champlain*, 1855
Graphite on paper 3 3/8 x 11 3/8
Dated and inscribed l.c. June 27, 1955/
Lake Champlain
Courtesy of William Vareika Fine Arts,
Newport, Rhode Island

5. *Pleasant Valley, Essex County*, 1855
Graphite on paper 4 15/16 x 11 7/8
Dated and inscribed l.r. Pleasant Valley/Essex
County, N.Y./June 29th 1855
Private collection

6. *Plains of North Elba*, 1855
Graphite on paper 4 1/8 x 12 1/4
Dated and inscribed l.l. Plains of North
Elba/Adirondack mts./July 2nd 1855
Private collection

7. *Indian Pass, Adirondacks*, 1855
Graphite on paper 10 7/8 x 8 1/4
Inscribed and dated l.c. Indian Pass—
Adirondack/July 3rd 1855
The Adirondack Museum 2000.2.1

8. *Schroon River*, 1855
Graphite on paper 5 3/4 x 11 3/4
Inscribed and dated l.l. Schroon River/
July 5th 1855
Private collection

9. *Pleasant Valley*, 1855
Graphite on paper 3 1/2 x 12
Inscribed l.l. Pleasant/Valley
Dated l.c. July 27th [or 29th]
Verso: part of another landscape
Private collection

10. *Essex Valley Adirondack Mountains*, 1855
Pencil on paper 4 7/8 x 11 7/8
Dated l.l. July 29th 1855
Private collection

11. *In the Adirondacks*, 1857
Oil on canvas 29 x 43 1/2
Signed and dated l.l. Wm T. Richards/1857.
The Adirondack Museum 69.53.1 (211)

12. *A View in the Adirondacks*, ca. 1857
Oil on canvas 30 1/4 x 44 l/4
Signed and inscribed l.r. Wm. T. Richards/Phil.
Henry Art Gallery, Faye G. Allen Center for the
Visual Arts

13. *Autumn in the Adirondacks*, 1857–58
Oil on canvas 24 1/8 x 36 l/2
Signed l.l. Wm. T. Richards
Private collection

14. *Lake George, opposite Caldwell*, 1857
Oil on canvas 19 x 27
Signed and dated l.r. Wm. T. Richards. 185[7]
Private collection

15. *Day Lilies by a Wooden Fence*, 1862
Graphite on paper 9 1/8 x 6
Dated l.l.c. June 26 1862
National Academy of Design, New York
Bequest of Mrs. William T. Richards

16. *The Adirondacks, Essex County*, ca. 1863
Pencil on paper 12 7/8 x 19 3/8
Unsigned
Brooklyn Museum of Art
Gift of Edith Ballinger Price 86.53.4

17. *Adirondack Sketchbook*, June 14–19, 1863
Graphite on paper, no cover, unbound sections
4 3/4 x 8
Inscribed with various sites Keene, Bald Mountain,
East Ausable River, Bennets Pond, Lake Placid,
Mt. McIntyre, Wilmington Notch, Whiteface
Mountain, Jay
Brooklyn Museum of Art
Gift of Edith Ballinger Price 75.15.5

18. *Plant Study: Elizabethtown*, 1863
Graphite on paper 4 5/8 x 6 3/4
Dated and inscribed l.l.
June 22/1863/Elizabethtown
Inscribed c.r. 3 ft high
Private collection

19. *Rock Cliffs*, 1863
Graphite on paper 9 5/8 x 6 1/8
Dated l.c. July 21st 1863
Iris & B. Gerald Cantor Center for Visual Arts at
Stanford University 1992.55.36
Gift of M. J. and A. E. van Löben Sels

20. *Indian Pass, Adirondacks*, 1866
Charcoal and white chalk 19 x 23
Signed and dated l.l. W.T.R./1866
Arnot Art Museum 84.15, Purchased in part with
funds from the Anderson-Evans Foundation, 1984

21. *Essex County in the Adirondacks*, 1862–66
Oil on paper 4 x 6
Unsigned
Private collection

22. *Elizabethtown*, 1862–66
Oil on paper 4 x 6 1/2
Unsigned
Private collection

23. *The Adirondack Mountains*, ca. 1864
Oil on paper 4 1/4 x 6 1/2
Unsigned
Inscribed verso: Adirondack Mts.
Private collection

24. *Adirondack Landscape*, 1864
Oil on canvas 22 x 31
Signed and dated l.r. Wm. T. Richards 1864
Private collection

25. *Bouquet Valley in the Adirondacks*, ca. 1864
Oil on canvas backed by panel 15 x 22
Signed l.r. Wm. T. Richards
Private collection

26. *John Brown's Grave (Sketch)*, ca. 1864
Oil on artist's board 9 x 14
Signed l.r. W. T. Richards
Private collection, courtesy of Caldwell Gallery,
Manlius, New York

27. *A Valley in the Adirondacks*, ca. 1864
from the Charlotte Cushman Album
Oil on paper (mounted on Masonite)
6 1/4 x 9 3/4
Signed l.r. W. T. Richards.
Private collection

28. Cover of the Charlotte Cushman Album, 1864
Full green morocco quarto with ivory bosses
Bound by Pawson and Nicholson, Philadelphia
Collection of James B. Cummins Jr.

29. *Autumn in the Adirondacks*, 1865
Oil on canvas 25 x 36
Signed, dated, and inscribed l.r. Wm. T.
Richards/Phila. 1865
Kenneth Lux Gallery

30. *The Bouquet Valley, Adirondacks*, 1866
Oil on canvas 25 x 42
Signed, dated, and inscribed l.l. Wm T.
Richards/Phil. 1866
Biggs Museum of American Art

31. *Whiteface Mountain, Lake Placid*, n.d.
Oil on canvas board 9 3/4 x 15 3/8
Unsigned
National Academy of Design, New York, Bequest
of Anna Richards Brewster, 1952

32. *Whiteface Mountain, Lake Placid*, 1904
Oil on board 9 1/2 x 15 1/2
Signed l.l. Wm T. Richards.
Private collection

33. *Lake Placid*, ca. 1904
Oil/gouache on board 9 7/8 x 15 5/8
Unsigned
Iris & B. Gerald Cantor Center for Visual Arts at
Stanford University 1992.55.205
Gift of M. J. and A. E. van Löben Sels

34. *Lake Placid*, ca. 1904
Oil/gouache on board 9 7/8 x 15 5/8
Unsigned
Iris & B. Gerald Cantor Center for Visual Arts at
Stanford University 1992.55.206
Gift of M. J. and A. E. van Löben Sels

35. *Lake Placid [looking south]*, ca. 1904
Watercolor on paper 5 1/4 x 8 3/8
Signed l.c. W. T. Richards
Private collection

36. *Curly Birch Camp, Lake Placid, New York*,
ca. 1904
Anna Richards Brewster (1870–1952)
Oil on canvas 15 x 11
Unsigned
Private collection

37. *Schroon Lake*, ca. 1846
Thomas Cole (1801–1848)
Oil on canvas 33 x 32
Signed l.c. TC
65.3.2 (101)

38. Untitled: Boulder and Trees, ca. 1858
Asher B. Durand (1796–1886)
Oil on canvas 25 x 20
Signed l.r. ABD
72.36.1 (281) Gift of Mrs. Douglas Delanoy

39. *Lake George*, 1856
John Frederick Kensett (1816–1872)
Oil on canvas 26 x 42
Signed l.r. JFK
65.79.1 (112)

40. Untitled: Boating Party on Lake George,
ca. 1867
Alfred Thompson Bricher (1837–1908)
Oil on canvas 26 x 48
Signed l.r. A. T. Bricher
82.4.1 (443)

41. *View from the Ruins of Fort George,
Lake George*, 1873
David Johnson (1827–1908)
Oil on canvas 16 x 28
Signed and dated l.r. DJ '73
2001.23 (562) Gift in memory of Klari Horvath
Erdoss and Bela K. Erdoss

42. *The Sacandaga River at Hadley, New York*, 1867
DeWitt Clinton Boutelle (1820–1884)
Oil on canvas 20 x 30
Signed l.l. Boutelle
90.2.1 (509)

43. *A Hunting Party in the Woods,/In the
Adirondack* [sic] *N.Y. State*, 1856
Frederick Rondel (1826–1892)
Oil on canvas 22 x 30
Signed l.r. F. Rondel
65.15.1 (104) Gift of The Shelburne Museum,
Shelburne, Vt., through the generosity of
J. Watson Webb

44. *Long Lake*, ca. 1855
James Cameron (1817–1882)
Oil on canvas 22 x 42
Signed l.c. J. Cameron
69.91 (213) Gift of Farrand Northrup Benedict Jr.

45. *A Twilight in the Adirondacks*, 1864
Sanford Robinson Gifford (1823–1880)
Oil on canvas 24 x 36
Signed l.r. S. R. Gifford
63.124.2 (90)

46. *A View of the Valley of Keene, Essex County*, 1851
J. A. Martin (n.d.)
Oil on canvas 16 x 20
Signed and dated l.r. J. A. Martin 1851
98.50.1 (548)

47. *Keene Valley, Adirondacks*, 1861
Joseph Vollmering (1810–1887)
Oil on canvas 16 x 22
Unsigned
97.48.1 (540) Gift of Richard T. Button

48. Untitled: Night Scene, 1861
William Hart (1823–1894)
Oil on canvas 8 x 16
Signed l.r. Wm. Hart
70.198.1 (233)

49. Untitled: View on Loon Lake, 1862
James M. Hart (1828–1901)
Oil on canvas 19 x 32
Signed l.r. J. M. Hart
67.220.6 (184)

50. *Mountain View on the Saranac*, 1868
Homer Dodge Martin (1836–1897)
Oil on canvas 30 x 56
Signed l.r. H. D. Martin
71.46.1 (262)

51. *Ausable Lake, Adirondack Mountains*, 1868
George Henry Smillie (1840–1921)
Oil on canvas 11 x 18
Signed l.r. Geo. H. Smillie
74.29.2 (377)

52. *Top of Giant's Leap, Adirondacks*, 1869
James David Smillie (1833–1909)
Watercolor on paper 20 x 13
Unsigned
62.9.1 (60) Gift of Mrs. Harold K. Hochschild

53. Untitled: Ausable River, ca. 1869
Samuel Colman (1832–1920)
Oil on canvas 30 x 40
Signed l.r. Sam. l Colman
72.160.3 (311) Gift of Harold K. Hochschild

54. Untitled: Wolf Jaw Mountain, 1863
Horace Wolcott Robbins Jr. (1842–1904)
Oil on canvas 13 x 22
Signed l.l. Robbins
74.292.1 (376)

55. *Village, Essex County, New York*, ca. 1867
Alexander Lawrie (1828–1917)
Oil on canvas 12 5/8 x 25
Signed and dated l.l. A. Lawrie/18[illegible]
95.22.1 (532) Purchase in memory of
Patricia Carroll Fitzgerald Mandel

56. *The Adirondack Mountains, near
Elizabethtown, Essex Co., N.Y. in 1866*
John Henry Dolph (1835–1903)
Oil on canvas 27 x 48
Signed l.l. J. H. Dolph
66.24.1 (117)

57. *Whiteface Mountain from Lake Placid, Essex
Co.*, 1873
Augustus Rockwell (1822–1882)
Oil on canvas 17 x 14
Signed on verso: Rockwell, Pt.
68.125.1 (197)

58. *Baker's Farm*, 1859
Eliphalet Terry (1826–1896)
Oil on canvas 19 x 30
Unsigned
L13.1998.1 Courtesy North Woods Club

59. *Still Hunting on the First Snow:
A Second Shot*, 1855
Arthur Fitzwilliam Tait (1819–1905)
Oil on canvas 54 x 76
Signed l.r. A. F. Tait
65.36.10 (110) Gift of Mr. and Mrs. Walter
Hochschild

60. *A Good Time Coming*, 1862
Arthur Fitzwilliam Tait (1819–1905)
Oil on canvas 20 x 30
Signed l.c. A. F. Tait
63.37.1 (76) Gift of Harold K. Hochschild

# Index